BRAUDE'S TREASURY OF WIT AND HUMOR FOR ALL OCCASIONS

Revised Edition

BRAUDE'S TREASURY OF WIT AND HUMOR FOR ALL OCCASIONS

Revised Edition

by
Jacob M. Braude

Revised by
Glenn Van Ekeren

PRENTICE HALL
Englewood Cliffs, New Jersey 07632

Prentice-Hall International (UK) Limited, *London*
Prentice-Hall of Australia Pty. Limited, *Sydney*
Prentice-Hall Canada, Inc., *Toronto*
Prentice-Hall Hispanoamericana, S.A., *Mexico*
Prentice-Hall of India Private Limited, *New Delhi*
Prentice-Hall of Japan, Inc., *Tokyo*
Simon & Schuster Asia Pte. Ltd., *Singapore*
Editora Prentice-Hall do Brasil, Ltda., *Rio de Janeiro*

© 1991 *by*
PRENTICE-HALL, Inc.
Englewood Cliffs, NJ

10 9 8 7 6 5 4 3

Library of Congress Cataloging-in-Publication Data

Braude, Jacob Morton
   [Treasury of wit and humor]
   Braude's Treasury of wit and humor / Jacob M. Braude ; revised by
Glenn Van Ekeren.—Rev. ed.
     p.   cm.
   Includes index.
   ISBN 0-13-093659-6
   1. American wit and humor. 2. Anecdotes.   I. Van Ekeren, Glenn.
II. Title.   III. Title: Treasury of wit and humor.
PN6162.B694   1991
818'.50208—dc20   91-12868
                                            CIP

ISBN 0-13-093659-6
ISBN 0-13-093667-7 PBK

PRENTICE HALL
BUSINESS & PROFESSIONAL DIVISION
A division of Simon & Schuster
Englewood Cliffs, New Jersey 07632

Printed in the United States of America

Introduction

While primarily slanted to the needs of the public speaker, this book can be a source of pleasure and entertainment to the man and woman who may be called upon to make a public utterance. There are hundreds of anecdotes, jokes and stories which follow that can be used over and over again to help you scintillate in your daily conversation. They comprise some of the best of thousands of items which I have managed to collect during the course of some fifty years of reading, clipping and filing.

I, myself, have dipped into this material literally thousands of times while preparing my own public speeches and writings and it is without reservation that I recommend it to the reader for the same purpose, because in making my selection I have always asked myself, "Can this be used with effect upon an audience and does it help to make a point that I am trying to put over?"

All of us have had the experience of trying desperately to reach back into the recesses of our memory for some story or anecdote to illustrate a given point and all too often that memory has failed us or has come up with an unsatisfactory substitute. In this book I have tried to build a never-failing addition to one's memory and have undertaken to make it readily accessible through the minutely detailed index which is part of the book itself. Here one will find titles, subject matter and also key words, which provide broad paths from which one can pinpoint the answer to a particular speaking or writing need.

Whoever makes use of this volume for the primary purpose for which it is intended is like the young man who always enters a movie theater with his eyes tightly shut; this, in turn, thereafter enables him to see in the dark and to find his seat. It has been my observation that too many public speakers seem to close their eyes to the need of brightening up their material with pertinent, illustrative anecdotes. The material in this book will be found to glow in the darkness of a dull or colorless presentation and thus bring it to life once again.

It is a good policy never to put one's listening audience in the position of the diner who asked of his waiter: "What have I done that they have kept me on bread and water for two hours?" With the material in this book you will be able to give your audience a gourmet's thought diet by flavoring your ideas with the wisdom and humor of others—always directly pertinent to the issue at hand.

With these few words I leave you on your own with the wish that you have happy hunting as you set forth in search of the story or anecdote that "just fits." My relationship with the material in this book is pretty much like that of the young lad who was riding horseback with his girl friend. As they stopped to rest, the two horses rubbed necks affectionately.

"Ah, me," said the lad, "that's what I'd like to do, too."

"Go ahead," said the girl, "it's *your* horse."

And I say to you about the material that follows: "Go ahead, friend. It's *yours* now. Read it, use it, and enjoy it."

Reviser Comments

You hold in your hands the revised edition of Jacob M. Braude's *Treasury of Wit and Humor*. Speakers, readers, and audiences have benefited for over 25 years from the humorous material contained in this original classic. Judge Braude's keen sense of humor and sensitivity to speakers and audiences alike have made this treasury the wonderful resource it is.

Even a timeless treasury of material such as this can benefit from periodic review and revision. As times change, so do the people, places, and things that add humor to our lives. What made an incident funny in 1955 or 1965, or, for that matter, 1985, may no longer get so much as a chuckle unless the audience can relate to the contents and details of the story. Given this reality, Braude's original effort deserves a standing ovation for withstanding the test of time.

I am indeed honored by Prentice Hall's invitation to update, revise, and fine-tune Judge Braude's masterpiece. Every effort has been made to maintain Braude's unique flair and yet address the interests of today's speakers and audiences.

Each entry was evaluated based on present-day applicability and receptivity. Language changes were inserted where gender demarcating was in question. Outdated material was updated or deleted while podium-tested new material was added to address a diversity of subject matters. I was careful to select from my own humor files funny material on relevant topics. Careful attention was given to every detail that would insure the continued success of this revision.

This book is not intended to make you a successful stand-up comedian. It does, however, provide a reservoir of resources for the beginner or seasoned speaker that will add a touch of flair to your next presentation, so the next time you need a one-liner, story, or definition to liven up your presentation, or want to develop an entirely humorous speech, the material is as nearby as the shelf you place this book on.

As a speaker myself, I know how important it is to be able to locate quickly and easily material that will fit a particular situation. Finding effective humorous material is no laughing matter when the success of your next speech depends on it. Therefore, we got serious about providing you a resource of humor. The revised *Treasury of Wit and Humor* features a cadre of timely topics.

We addressed new areas such as:

* Athletics
* Attitude
* Children
* Customer Service
* Economics
* Hospitals
* Lifestyles
* Listening
* Money
* Office Humor
* Presidential Humor
* Problems
* Professions
* Religion
* School
* Self-Concept
* Speaking
* Winning/Losing
* Work

This is just a small sample of the extensive list of new topics. In addition, several existing topics were expanded upon and the humorous definitions section now includes over 360 entries. Quotes and stories from the lives of such people as Ronald Reagan, Erma Bombeck, Yogi Berra, Bob Hope, Dan Quayle, Archie Bunker, Johnny Carson, and George Bush will add zest to your next presentation. The new *Treasury of Wit and Humor* is a veritable goldmine of valuable nuggets and unlimited resources—and the best part is, it works! Choosing from the over 1,400 power-packed entries will generate laughter in practically any situation.

"There are three things that are real," said John F. Kennedy. "God, human folly, and laughter. The first two are beyond comprehension. So, we must do what we can with the third." We have "done what we can" to make humor a powerful communication tool. Used as is or modified for your situation, this material will assist you in gaining the attention of your audience, creating rapport, and making your message a memorable one. So no matter how frequently or seldom you speak, no matter how often you stand before new audiences or old friends, you no longer need to be without fresh, rousing, successful material.

This book is funny! While reading it, you might even laugh to yourself (and thereby reduce the effects of stress in your life), find stories to break up the monotony of a stuffy workplace, get ideas for motivating people, or even come across material that will liven up the next dinner party you attend. As Victor Borge said, "Laughter is the shortest distance between two people." Shared laughter enhances your life and your relationships, and that's no joke.

Remember the words of Laurence Peter: "There are three rules for creating humor, but unfortunately no one knows what they are." Get creative. Use your imagination. There are no hard-and-fast rules on how to use this material. Select those stories or one-liners which you believe are not only funny but also make a point about the subject you wish to address. Remember, when you touch the funny bone of the human mind, the door of the mind will be open to new and enlightening information. Grab people's attention through laughter and you will find humor to be an essential element in your speaking repertoire.

Contents

Absent-mindedness

1. An absent-minded man tied a string around his finger in the early afternoon to remind him when he got home that there was something he wanted to be sure to do. After dinner, while reading his paper, he noticed the string but couldn't remember why he put it there. He decided if he sat up long enough, the reason for the string would come to him. And surely enough, around two o'clock in the morning it did—he wanted to go to bed early that night.

Accuracy

2. A stranger entered the building and asked a boy standing in the lobby, "Can you tell me where Mr. Smith lives?"

The young man smiled and replied pleasantly, "Yes, sir. I'll show you."

Six flights up the boy pointed out a room as that belonging to Mr. Smith. The man pounded on the door repeatedly and, after no response, commented, "He's not here."

"Oh, no, sir," replied the boy. "Mr. Smith was downstairs waiting in the lobby."

3. A tourist was visiting New Mexico. While gazing at the dinosaur bones that were everywhere, he met an elderly Indian who acted as an unofficial guide.

"How old are these bones?" asked the tourist.

"Exactly one hundred million and three years old," was the Indian's reply.

"How can you be so definite?" inquired the tourist.

"Oh, a geologist told me they were one hundred million years old," replied the Indian, "and that was exactly three years ago."

Achievement

4. *Bob:* "Can you do anything that other people can't?"
Herb: "Why, yes. I can read my own handwriting."

5. A bright junior executive struggled to achieve company quotas assigned to her. While at lunch one day, she asked her senior mentor how she managed the multiple priorities in her job.

"I learned a long time ago," responded the seasoned veteran, "that there are basically three ways to get things done. You can do it yourself, get someone else to do it, or ask your children not to do it."

6. Gretchen Alexander refused to allow her blindness to limit her life experiences. She mastered archery, golf, softball, sailing, and water skiing as well as a number of other activities her sighted friends had yet to learn.

Speaking before a group of high school students about her achievements, one student asked if there was anything she wouldn't try. "I've decided to never sky dive," she answered. "It would scare the heck out of my dog."

7. The story is told of a community-minded business person being honored for his contributions to the community. Grateful citizens gathered for a testimonial dinner to thank the man for his giving spirit. In introducing the well-respected man, the Chamber of Commerce President shared a long list of his accomplishments, including being president of a large manufacturing company, possessing several real estate holdings, having spearheaded a host of economic development projects, and an exhausting list of voluntary involvements.

"Your support is overwhelming," said the honored man when he began to speak. "Many of you are well aware of my accomplishments and that not one of them would have been possible without your help. For I came to this community with the clothes I was wearing and a paper bag containing all my worldly belongings."

At the close of the speech, a young admirer asked, "What was in the bag?"

"My million dollar inheritance," came the reply.

Admiration

8. A young American woman stood before Beethoven's piano in a Vienna museum. Presently she struck off a few discordant notes. "I suppose," she said to the attendant, "that many noted musicians have inspected this instrument."

"Oh, yes," replied the man. "Recently Paderewski was here."

"Paderewski!" exclaimed the visitor. "Certainly he must have played something wonderful."

"On the contrary; he did not feel worthy to touch it."

Advancement

9. There are people who spend their entire lives working with an attitude not unlike Snoopy, the cherished Peanuts cartoon pet. Snoopy sat droopy-eyed at the entrance of his dog house lamenting, "Yesterday I was a dog. Today I'm a dog. Tomorrow I'll probably still be a dog. SIGH. There's so little hope for advancement!"

Advertising

10. *Want ad:* Secretary wants job; no bad habits; willing to learn.

11. If advertising can be accused of making people live beyond their means, so can matrimony.

12. A manufacturer said he was going to cut down on his advertising to save money. To which his salesperson replied: "You might as well stop your watch to save time."

13. A man who lives in the suburbs of Los Angeles and who works in the advertising department of a large metropolitan newspaper had never been able to figure out the deferential attitude, bordering on awe, of the children in the block towards him. Recently, he was walking around the block for a little stroll and he came upon a group of little boys discussing the newest American satellite as it hurtled through orbital space around the earth. As he paused to say hello to the youngsters, everything suddenly became clear when one of the boys said to him: "Are you really a space salesperson?"

14. Jay Leno is concerned about truth in advertising. He says a lot of products are not as good as advertised. He says he bought a tube of Krazy Glue and the label fell off.

Age

15. The age of some people is like the speedometer on a used car—you know it's set back but you don't know how far.

16. *Ticket Seller:* "You will have to pay for an adult ticket for your child, lady. He's over twelve."
Movie Goer: "How can he be over twelve when I've only been married ten years."
Ticket Seller: "I'm sorry ma'm, I just collect fares—not confessions."

17. A pretty girl came to a roulette table at Las Vegas with a $100 bill and explained to a group of admirers that she could not decide which number to bet it on.
"Why don't you play it on your age?" one of the men suggested.
"That's a good idea—I'll do it," the girl said, and she placed the $100 on 22. The wheel spun and finally came to a stop at 28.
"Oh, no!!" the girl gasped and fell to the floor in a faint.

18. "Your name, please?" asked the registration officer.
"Matilda Brown," answered the woman.
"And your age?" he pursued.
"Have the Misses Hill next door, given you their ages?" she asked, hesitantly.
"No," said the officer.
"Well, then, I'm the same age as they."
"That will do," said the officer. Then, proceeding to fill out the form, he wrote, "Matilda Brown, as old as the Hills."

19. James Russell Lowell, when passing a building in the outskirts of Boston, noticed a sign which read: "Home for Incurable Children." To an accompanying friend, he remarked, "They'll get me in there some day."

20. Ronald Reagan was sixty-nine years old when he ran for President in 1980. Despite continual criticism, he won the election and never passed up an opportunity to use humor when referring to his age.

Reagan delighted audiences with comments about his age. On one occasion, he said, "And I want to say that I don't mind at all any of the jokes or remarks about my age, because Thomas Jefferson made a comment about the Presidency and age. He said that one should not worry about one's exact chronological age in reference to his ability to perform one's task. And ever since he told me that, I stopped worrying."

Perhaps one of the most memorable events concerning his age occurred during a televised debate between Ronald Reagan and Walter Mondale in the 1984 Presidential Campaign. Reagan was sure the issue of age had been put to rest during his four years of Presidency. However, a reporter surfaced the issue by asking Reagan if he was too old to serve another term. Reagan was prepared and responded in such a way as to quiet even his greatest critics. "I'm not going to inject the issue of age into this campaign," Reagan began. "I am not going to exploit for political gain my opponent's youth and inexperience."

Aging

21. You're getting old when you don't care where your spouse goes, just so you don't have to go along.

22. A white-haired old man approached his doctor and said: "Doctor, I'm slowly going nuts over women. Is there any way to speed it up?"

23. Careful grooming and a smooth paint job will take 20 years off a person's true age. But you can't fool a long flight of stairs.

24. In the post office a stranger saw the local patriarch sitting on a park bench across the street, whistling. A bystander informed him that the old fellow already had passed his hundredth birthday. Impressed, the man exclaimed, "That's amazing!"

"We don't see nothin' amazin' about it 'round here," was the laconic reply. "All he's done is grow old—and he took longer to do that than most people would!"

25. It is said that when Konrad Adenauer, former West German Chancellor, was laid up with the grippe, he chafed at his doctor and said he had to get better because he was scheduled to make an official trip abroad.

"I'm not a magician," said the doctor. "I can't make you young again."

To which Adenauer is reported to have replied: "I'm not asking that. I don't want to become young again; all I want is to go on getting old."

26. Sir Winston Churchill, whose fondness for drink was well known, was scheduled to make a speech before a small gathering.

The chairperson introduced him by saying: "If all the spirits consumed by Sir Winston were poured into this room, it would reach up to here on the wall."

He drew a line with his finger at about level with his eyes.

Churchill got up to speak. He glanced at the imaginary line on the wall. He looked up at the ceiling, and made a mathematical calculation with his fingers. Then he sighed and said, "Ah, so much to be done, and so little time in which to do it."

America—Americanism

27. If you want your father to take care of you, that's paternalism. If you want your mother to take care of you, that's maternalism. If you want Uncle Sam to take care of you, that's Socialism. If you want your comrades to take care of you, that's Communism. But if you want to take care of yourself, that's Americanism.

Ancestry

28. "I want a dog of which I can be proud," said Mrs. Newlyrich. "Does that one have a good pedigree?"

"Oh, yes," declared the kennel owner, "if he could talk, he wouldn't speak to either of us."

29. The lady was trying to impress those at the party. "My family's ancestry is very old," she said. "It dates back to the days of King John of England." Then turning to a lady sitting quietly in a corner she asked condescendingly: "How old is your family, my dear?"

"Well," said the woman with a quiet smile, "I can't really say. All our family records were lost in the Flood."

Anger

30. A man is never in worse company than when he flies into a rage and is beside himself.

Anti-climactic

31. Orville and Wilbur Wright's efforts to get their new flying machine off the ground were met with continual failure. Finally one December day at Kitty Hawk, Orville achieved an historical milestone. He did what no one had ever done before and the moment deserved celebration. The two brothers quickly wired their sister Katherine, "We did it. We have actually flown in the air 120 feet. Will be home for Christmas." Excited about her brothers' achievement, Katherine delivered the message to the local newspaper editor. He glanced at the wired message and said, "This is nice news for the family—having both boys home for Christmas."

Antique–Antiques

32. A lady, traveling in a group determined to outdo one another in their search for antiques, one day called upon the leader and excitedly remarked: "I came across something marvelous. An archaeologist friend sent me the very cup from which Socrates drank the hemlock."

"Are you sure it's authentic?" gasped the pace-setter.

"Authentic?" repeated the woman. "Why when they dug it up it was marked 350 B.C."

Appearances

33. A couple was driving through town one summer afternoon. The weather was hot and the windows were rolled up. "Honey," he said, "please open the windows."

"Are you crazy!" she exclaimed. "And let our neighbors driving in the next lane know our car isn't air-conditioned?"

34. Two girls at the beach were admiring the passing scene, which included an athletic chap, who was strutting his best.

"That's my kind," said one.

"Well, I don't know," the other replied. "I had a friend who married a man who owned a two-car garage, but he just keeps a bicycle in it."

Appreciation

35. A woman experiencing appreciation depravation decided to do something special for her thirteenth wedding anniversary. She called the flower shop and ordered thirteen long-stem roses along with a card that read: "I love you! Bill." When the flowers arrived at the house, her husband Bill was curious about who had actually sent the flowers. For twenty-one days, Bill had no idea who would send his wife flowers and sign the card in his name. Then on the twenty-second day, the mystery was solved. His charge card bill arrived.

36. A man attending a seminar on interpersonal relationships became convinced of the need for him to begin showing appreciation to people. His family seemed like an appropriate place to start. So on his way home, he picked up a dozen long-stem roses and a delicious box of chocolates. This was going to be a real surprise, and he was excited to begin showing his wife how much he appreciated her.

Arriving home, he walked up to the front door, rang the doorbell, and waited for his wife to answer. Immediately, upon seeing him, she began to cry.

"What's the matter honey?" asked the confused husband.

"Oh, it's been a terrible day," she responded. "First, Tommy tried to flush his diaper down the toilet, then the dishwasher quit working, Sally came home from school with her legs all scratched, and now . . . and now you come home drunk."

Apprehension

37. When John Glenn, the first U.S. Astronaut in space, was asked about his thoughts just before taking off into space, he responded: "I looked around me and suddenly realized that everything had been built by the lowest bidder."

Approval

38. It was a blistering-hot afternoon as the senator stood through the sun-roof in his chauffeur-driven limousine orating at length to the uneasy crowd of voters gathered at the town square. Before he had completed his speech, his driver began pulling away. Immediately the crowd broke into applause, accompanied by cheering and shouting.

With the shouts fading in the distance, the senator settled into his seat and remarked to a man accompanying him: "You know something? I'm not sure whether they were applauding me or my driver."

Argument

39. A husband made an investment, against his wife's better judgment, and lost a large sum of money. The incident resulted in a major, unresolved spat at the dinner table. Later in the evening, when both had cooled, the husband approached his wife. "Just so I'm clear in the future," he began, "would you kindly tell me the difference between your saying 'I told you so' and 'I'm not going to say I told you so?'"

Arithmetic

40.   Several young clerical workers were riding down in the elevator for their coffee break. Forgetting completely the warnings of her high school math teacher, one new recruit complained: "That job I got. Is it ever strict? If the total is wrong, it's all wrong!"

41.   "When are you going back to school, Tom?"
"I'm not going back, 'cause my teacher's gone crazy."
"Gone crazy?"
"Yes. One day she told us that four and one are five, and today she says that two and three make five."

42.   "I can't figure it out," said the small boy trying to get his father to help him with his arithmetic. "If a carpenter was paid $13 a day, how much did he earn in four days?"
"No wonder you can't figure it out," replied the father. "That's not arithmetic—that's ancient history."

43.   The harried coach pleaded with the professor who had flunked his prize tackle to give the boy another chance. Finally the professor agreed and did give his boy a special makeup exam.
The next day the coach again anxiously queried the professor. "How did Jones do?"
"I'm sorry," said the professor. "It's hopeless. Look at this . . . $7 \times 5 = 33$."
"But gosh, Professor," said the coach, "give him a break. He only missed it by one."

Armed Forces

44.   If you think old soldiers just fade away, try getting into your old Army uniform.

45.   *Johnnie:* "I would rather be a general than a private. Generals don't have to fight for their medals."

46.   A soldier leaving an army base was overheard saying to a comrade: "This has got to be love at first sight. I'm on an eight-hour pass."

47. *Supply officer:* "How does your new uniform fit?"
Recruit: "The jacket isn't bad, but the trousers are just a little loose around the armpits."

48. *Postmaster:* "I'm sorry, but I can't cash this money order unless you have some identification. Have you friends in camp?"
Soldier: "Not me: I'm the camp's bugler."

49. The sergeant was explaining some important points to a squad of recruits on the rifle range.
"This type of bullet will penetrate two feet of solid wood," he said. "So remember to keep your heads down."

50. "Look here, private, this man beside you on this fatigue detail is doing twice the work you are."
"I know, sarge. That's what I've been telling him for the last hour, but he won't slow down."

51. The major who received a complaint about the issue of bread snapped angrily, "If Napoleon had had that bread in Russia, he would have eaten it with the greatest relish."
"Yes, sir," spoke up the sergeant, "but it was fresh then."

52. The draftee was awakened roughly by his platoon sergeant after the rookie's first night in the army barracks.
"It's four-thirty!" roared the sergeant.
"Four-thirty!" gasped the recruit. "Man, you'd better get to bed. We've got a big day tomorrow!"

53. An officer in the South Pacific who had been overseas sixteen months received a letter from his wife telling about a prayer their four-year-old daughter made: "Dear Lord, please send me a baby brother so we will have something to surprise Daddy with when he gets home."

54. An applicant for employment gave as his reason for leaving his previous job, which was that of a temporary sorter at the post office: "Done all the work."
He had also served in the Army, and to the formal question: "Why did you leave the Forces?" he replied: "Won the War."

55. A naval officer fell overboard. He was rescued by a deck hand. The officer asked how he could reward him.

"The best way, sir," said the deck hand, "is to say nothing about it. If the other fellows knew I'd pulled you out, they'd chuck me in."

56. A sergeant in charge of the new recruits ordered: "Men, when I blow the whistle, I want you to shoot at will."

At that moment one very frightened young man ran across the grounds out of sight.

"Who was that? Where's he going?" bellowed the sergeant.

"That was Will," replied one of the recruits.

57. Sergeant-Major's golden rules for new recruits detailed for duty in the Officers' Mess:

"If it moves, salute it.

If it doesn't move, sweep it up.

If it's too big to sweep up, pick it up.

If it's too big to pick up, paint it."

58. The old colonel had put in forty long years under Army routine, and now he was being retired. He took his orderly with him as a servant, and gave him strict instructions:

"Now, George, each morning at five o'clock sharp you wake me up and say, 'Time for the parade, sir,' and then I'll say, 'Damn the parade!' and turn over and go back to sleep."

59. An Army veteran passed through a small town and saw evidence of amazing shooting. On trees, walls, fences, and barns were numerous bull's-eyes with the bullet hole in the exact center. He asked to meet the remarkable shooter.

The expert turned out to be a young boy with his first BB gun. "This is the most wonderful shooting I've ever seen," said the Army veteran. "How in the world do you do it?"

"Easy as pie. I shoot first and draw the circle afterwards."

60. "Now watch out for the colonel, because he's coming to inspect the post," said the sergeant, as he marched off and left O'Brien to his first outpost duty. After an hour the sergeant returned. "Colonel been here yet?" he asked.

O'Brien saying "No," the sergeant again departed for an hour, returning with the same query.

Then, at last, the colonel did appear.

"Do you know who I am?" he asked O'Brien.

"Shure, an' I don't at all," replied the recruit.

"I am the colonel."

"Faith, an' you'll catch it, then! The sergeant's been asking fer you twice already."

61.   The lady was not aware that her drive had carried her into an army maneuvers area. As she approached a small bridge, a sentry stopped her and said, "Sorry, but you can't drive across this bridge. It has just been demolished." Leaving her dumbfounded, for the bridge was in perfect repair, he walked off.

As shc sat pondering the possibility that the sentry was insane, another soldier approached. "Young man," she asked, "can you tell me any reason why I can't cross that bridge?"

"Lady," he replied soberly, "I can't tell you a thing. I've been dead for two days."

62.   Two harassed-looking privates were staggering across the barrack square from the direction of the kitchens with a huge steaming cauldron slung between them. The most officious, most interfering officer in the whole regiment spotted them from his window and straightaway sallied forth. "Hi, there, you men—put that down." They did so. "Get me a ladle," ordered the officer. "B-b-but, sir—" stammered one of the privates. "Don't query an order," snapped the officer. "Do as you are told. Get me a ladle." A ladle was duly obtained. The officer dipped it into the cauldron, brought it out full, blew on the contents, swallowed them. His face changed. "Call that soup?" he demanded, fiercely. "N-n-no, sir," came the stammering reply, "it's the water we've just washed the dishes in."

63.   A draftee on his way to training camp asked another draftee. "Do you happen to have a match?"

"Sure," was the second draftee's reply. "But I'm making sure not to give you any."

"But why?" was the startled query from the first recruit.

"Well," said the second, "we'll get to talking, and if we get to talking, we'll wind up as buddies. And if we're buddies, we'll get into the same tent and the same squad; then we'll both volunteer to go for special missions. Maybe we'll even get a dangerous night job; and we'll have to use flashlights. And if the flashlights should happen to go out some dark night in enemy territory, I sure don't want to be stranded with someone who doesn't even carry matches!"

Art

64.   The newly rich woman was going through a "culture" routine and at this particular moment was standing in front of a painting at New York's famous Metropolitan Museum. It was a beautiful oil of a ragged but happy vagabond.

"Well!" exclaimed the woman indignantly, "How do you like that? Too broke to buy a decent suit of clothes, but he can afford to go out and get his portrait painted."

65.   A tiny but dignified old lady was among a group looking at an art exhibition in a newly opened gallery recently. Suddenly one contemporary painting caught her eye.

"What on earth," she inquired of the artist standing nearby, "is that?"

He smiled condescendingly. "That, my dear lady, is supposed to be a mother and her child."

"Well, then," snapped the little old lady, "why isn't it?"

Art, Modern

66.   Two teenagers on a tour of a modern art gallery found themselves alone in a room of modern sculpture. Staring at the twisted pipes, broken glass, and tangled shapes, one of them said, "Let's get out of here before they accuse us of wrecking this place."

67.   An American GI who met Pablo Picasso in Paris told the artist that he didn't like modern paintings because they weren't realistic. Picasso made no immediate reply. A few minutes later the soldier showed him a snapshot of his girl friend.

"My word," said Picasso, "is she *really* as small as all that?"

Athletics

68.   A high school track coach was having difficulty motivating his team to perform at their best. The team developed a distinct reputation of coming in last at every track meet they entered.

One factor contributing to this less than successful program was the coach's pep talk tactics. His most effective, inspiring tool was to tell his team to "keep turning left and hurry back."

69.   Susie had an encouraging soccer coach. At the end of the first week of practice, Susie asked her coach how she was doing. "Just fine," the coach responded. "You are the best of my five worst players."

70.   Joe was quite an athlete. He used to play tailback on his college football team. Every time Joe started to go on the field, his coach would holler: "Joe, get your 'tail back' on the bench."

71.   Mary wanted to play on her school's basketball team. Unfortunately, she was so uncoordinated, she couldn't even clap for those who did play.

72.   Spring football training is a grueling affair. A winter of eating popcorn, watching television, and limited physical exercise makes getting back in shape painful. The first afternoon back, a tough head coach was putting the team through a calisthenics routine. Push-ups, sit-ups, and jumping jacks were followed by the bicycle. This exercise requires a player to lay on his back, legs up in the air, and move them as if you were riding a bicycle. "Is there a problem?" the coach asked one motionless player. "No problem," he replied. "I'm coasting."

Attention

73.   A professor who had taught for many years was counseling a young teacher. "You will discover," he said, "that in nearly every class, there will be a youngster eager to argue. Your first impulse will be to silence him, but I advise you to think carefully before doing so. He probably is the only one listening."

16

Attire

74. A wife bought her husband a new tie for his birthday. "I wonder what would go best with it," she asked, after he had opened the package.

The husband eyed the violet-colored horror, and exclaimed, "A beard!"

75. A rather stout woman visited her foot doctor. After he pried her foot loose from a dainty shoe, he asked her what her trouble was.

"It seems my feet are always swollen," she complained. "I wonder what causes this."

The doctor glanced at her feet, then at the shoes. "Well," he mused, "it could be pride in accomplishing the impossible."

Attitude

76. A generally negative lady reacted to the minister's message that every day is a great day. "This is the day the Lord has made," he said, "let us rejoice and be glad in it."

"What do you mean I should be joyful?" the lady provoked. "It is a lousy day. It has been raining in sheets most of the morning, the rain ruined my hair and the fog is becoming so dense I won't be able to see my way home. In my opinion, this is a good-for-nothing day. Tell me," she continued, "what is there to be joyful about today?"

A smile flashed across the minister's face as he responded, "Well, look at it this way. Today is holding yesterday and tomorrow together."

77. The summer of 1987 brought devastating tornadoes to the Minneapolis area. Local news stations reported massive damage and revealed the despair of emotionally distraught citizens. One reporter captured a slightly different slant in the aftermath. The paper pictured a man standing by his car, which had been crushed by a fallen tree. He was smiling, waving at people driving by, and holding a sign which read, "new-style compact car."

Authorship

78. "Why do you insist on calling him a pharmacist when you know he's an author?"

"Because every book he writes is a drug on the market."

79. A prisoner in a state penitentiary wrote a crime story and sent it to a magazine editor with this note: "The facts in this story are true, only the names have been changed to protect the guilty."

80. Novelist Sinclair Lewis was to lecture a group of college students who planned literary careers. Lewis opened his talk by saying:

"How many of you really intend to be writers?"

All hands went up.

"In that case," said Lewis, returning his notes to his pocket, "my advice to you is to go home and write."

With that, he left the room.

Awards

81. Upon accepting an award, Jack Benny once remarked, "I really don't deserve this. But I have arthritis and I don't deserve that either."

Bachelorhood

82. The bachelor's attractive new housekeeper tiptoed into the study and asked apologetically, "Sir, shall I clean your stove and sweep your porch now?"

"Margie," said the bachelor, "in this house we are all for one and one for all. You do not say 'your stove' or 'your porch' or 'your chair.' Instead you say 'our stove' or 'our porch' or 'our chair.'"

That evening Margie served a splendid dinner to the bachelor and his boss and the boss' daughter, whom the bachelor was anxious to impress.

Margie was late in serving the last course and she rushed into the dining room and excitedly announced: "I'm sorry I was late, sir, but I was upstairs chasing a mouse from under 'our bed.'"

Backfire

83. A young man looking for a seat on a crowded commuter walked to the last car and cried in a loud voice: "All change here. This car isn't going."

With exclamations the passengers cleared the car, and the young man sat down, made himself comfortable and waited—and waited.

Finally the station agent appeared. "You the smart young man who said this car wasn't going?"

"Yep," replied the clever one.

"Well," said the agent, "it isn't. You sounded so much like a director, they just uncoupled the car."

Baldness

84. *Small boy in barber's chair:* "I want my hair cut like my daddy's—with a hole on top."

85. There are three ways in which a man can wear his hair: parted, unparted, departed.

Bank—Banks—Banking

86. *Secretary:* "I think I know what's wrong with this country!"

Bank executive: "And what's that?"

Secretary: "We're trying to run America with only one vice-president."

87. A wealthy Texas oil tycoon cashed a huge personal check which came back from the bank with "INSUFFICIENT FUNDS" stamped across its face. Beneath the stamped words was the handwritten notation: "Not you . . . us."

88. Wanting to borrow some money to make a six-month tour of Europe, a man went to the bank where he had done business for years. The bank refused the loan.

He went to another bank and obtained the loan without any difficulty. Then he bought a five-pound fish, had it wrapped, and put it in his safe-deposit box at the first bank as he joyfully left town for six months.

89. The burglars had tied and gagged the bank cashier after extracting the combination to the safe and had herded the other employees into a separate room under guard. After they rifled the safe and were about to leave the cashier made desperate pleading noises through the gag. Moved by curiosity one of the burglars loosened the gag.

"Please!" whispered the cashier, "take the books, too: I'm $6,500 short."

Barber—Barber shop

90. "Your dog likes to watch you cut hair, doesn't he?" "It ain't that. Sometimes I snip off a bit of ear."

91. *Customer:* "I want a close shave."

Barber: "You just had one."

Customer: "How's zat?"

Barber: "That big guy who walked in just as you took your hand off the manicurist's knee is her husband."

92. A man walked into the barber's and asked for a shave. The barber's young assistant spoke up: "May I try shaving him? It'll be good practice."

"All right—go ahead," replied his boss doubtfully. "But be careful. Don't cut yourself."

93. A barber with a bad case of "morning after the night before" shakes nicked the customer he was shaving. The customer commented, "You see what too much liquor will do to you?"

"Yeah," replied the barber, "it sure makes your skin tender."

94. Sam, the barber, seemed a little jumpy and it made his customer nervous. "Sam," he said, "what happens if you cut a customer? Does the boss get sore?"

"Yes, he does," Sam replied. "He makes us pay a dollar for every cut we give a customer—but I don't care, I had a good day at the races yesterday."

Bargain—Bargains

95. *Fond parent to little boy:* "How much is two and two, son?"

Little boy: "Six."

Fond parent: "No, son, that's wrong. The answer is four."

Little boy: "I know what the answer is, father, but I just wanted to hear you bargain."

96. An elderly lady stepped up to the ticket window in the airport and asked, "How much is a ticket to Cleveland?"

"That's two hundred and forty nine dollars," replied the agent.

The elderly lady turned to the little girl beside her and said, "I guess we may as well buy our tickets here. I've asked at all these windows, and they are the same price everywhere."

Beauty

Behavior

97.   Little monkeys grow up to be big monkeys; little pigs grow up to be big pigs; but people, wonderful people, can grow up to be either.

98.   "I noticed that your daughter didn't get home until two this morning. My daughter, Shirley, was in by midnight."
"I know, but you see, my daughter walked home."

99.   A Broadway playboy decided to reform. The first week he cut out cigarettes. The second week he cut out booze. The third week he cut out dating. And the fourth week he cut out paper dolls.

100.   *Millie:* "I went out last night with a Southerner. He took me to dinner and dancing and was a perfect gentleman. Then he took me home in a cab."
Lillie: "What happened then?"
Millie: "He got a bit Northern."

101.   A newspaper was running a competition to discover the most high-principled, sober, well-behaved local citizen. Among the entries came one which read:
"I don't smoke, touch intoxicants or gamble. I am faithful to my wife and never look at another woman. I am hard-working, quiet and obedient. I never go to the movies or the theater, and I go to bed early every night and rise with the dawn. I attend chapel regularly every Sunday without fail.
"I've been like this for the past three years. But just wait until next spring, when they let me out of here!"

Bet—Bets—Betting. See also Gambling

102.   And then there's the touching story of the young man who said to his girl, "I bet you wouldn't marry me."
The story goes that she not only called his bet but raised him five.

103.   The bookie slowly counted out the money into the old lady's wrinkled hands.

"Lady," he said, "I just don't understand. However did you manage to pick the winner?"

The old lady patted her white locks in place. She looked a little bewildered.

"Really," she said, "I don't know myself. I just stick a pin in the paper and, well, there it is."

The bookie took a deep breath.

"That's all very well, lady," he cried. "But how on earth did you manage to pick four winners yesterday afternoon?"

"Oh," replied the old lady, "that was easy. You see, I used a fork."

Bible, The

104.   A woman was mailing the Old Family Bible to a brother in a distant city.

Postal clerk: "Does this package contain anything breakable?"

Lady: "Only the Ten Commandments."

105.   A group of executives got into a heated discussion about the Bible. Each one claimed they were more knowledgeable than the other. Finally, one executive challenged another, "I'll bet you don't even know the Lord's Prayer."

"Oh, that's easy," the other responded. "It's 'now I lay me down to sleep . . .'"

"Wow," the first executive said. "You are a lot more knowledgeable than I thought."

Blame

106.   Everyone needs a spouse because there are a number of things that go wrong that one can't blame on the government.

107.   A government census-taker was questioning an old-timer about his home town. "How many people live in this town?" he wanted to know.

" 'Bout four thousand people and it's been that way for twenty-five years," was the reply.

"You mean to tell me," said the census-taker, "that there were four thousand people here twenty-five years ago and only four thousand now? Haven't any people moved in—any babies been born here?"

"There sure have been babies born," cackled the old-timer. "Trouble is, that every time a baby is born, somebody leaves town."

Boastfulness

108.   Composing a letter to the president of the firm, which he felt he so ably represented, the egotistical young salesperson dictated to a stenographer:

"I feel that you should know, sir, that in order to obtain the above-mentioned contract, I found it necessary to employ every ounce of my personal charm and magnetism, my diplomacy and flawless tact. However, I am now pleased to report that my untiring efforts were crowned with success."

Gently the steno asked, "Crowtation marks on that last paragraph?"

109.   An old master sergeant, a veteran of three wars, was hard put to keep a brash teenage recruit in his place. Although the youngster bragged, he had a disconcerting knack of making good his boasts.

Marched to the rifle range, he announced that he was the best shot in the rookie unit—and lived up to it by outshooting the other recruits by a large margin. That night in the barracks, everyone suffered through his detailed account of how "I set a new range record."

Turning to his sergeant, the boastful youngster remarked: "Bet you didn't shoot that well when you first joined up, sarge."

After a pause, the sergeant replied: "No, son, I didn't. But when I first shot, there was somebody shooting back."

110.   Several hunters were sitting around bragging about the dogs they owned. Noting that an elderly native was listening intently, they laid it on thick.

"Take my setter," said one man. "When I send him to the store for eggs, he refuses to accept them unless they're fresh. What a nose that dog has!'"

"That's nothing," boasted another. "My springer goes out for cigars and refuses to accept any but my favorite brand. Not only that, he won't smoke any until he gets home and I offer him one."

"Say, old-timer," said another man turning to the native, "did you ever hear of any dogs as smart as ours?"

"Just one—my brother's dog," was the reply. "I think he's a bit smarter."

"How?" he was asked.

"Well," replied the native, "he runs the store where your dogs trade."

Book—Books

111.   The student approached the desk of the librarian and began searching her handbag for a note she had taken in class. Not finding it, she said hastily, "I want to take out the book called *The Red Boat.*"

The library assistant came back to her after a few minutes and said, "I'm sorry but we do not have a book by that title."

"I must have made a mistake," the girl replied. "I believe it was *The Scarlet Launch.*"

Again the library assistant came back and this time, trying to be helpful, suggested, "Could it be *The Scarlet Letter* by Hawthorne that you want?"

"No. It's not about a letter. It's about a boat," the girl said. And then her face brightened as she found her notes. "I have it written down," she spoke happily. "It is the *Ruby Yacht* by a man named Omar something or other."

Borrowing

112.   *Prospective borrower to banker:* "Now I'll need two thousand more . . . I bet my associate two grand that you'd turn me down."

113.   *Husband:* "Darling, don't you think you're being a wee bit extravagant? You've had four electric fans running all day."

Bride: "Don't worry about it, dearest. They're not our fans; I borrowed them from the neighbors."

114.   A fellow was endeavoring to borrow some money from a friend. The friend wanted to know why he didn't use his own money, and the fellow explained that everything he had was in a joint account. "But you can draw money from a joint account," volunteered his friend.

"Not this joint account," explained the financially destitute man. "The joint account is in the name of my parents."

Brevity

115.   The rookie reporter was told to keep his copy short and stick to the bare facts. Sent on his first accident story, he turned in this copy:

"S. White looked up the elevator shaft to see if the car was on its way down. It was. Age 45."

116.   The lesson in newspaper work is constantly "Be brief!" If that order can be given picturesquely, so much the better and it will not be forgotten.

A certain beginner in journalism picked up in a southern town what seemed to him a "big story." He hurried to the telegraph office and queried the editor of his newspaper: "Column story on—. Shall I send?"

The answer arrived promptly: "Send 600 words."

This to the enthusiastic correspondent was depressing. "Can't be told in less than 1,200," he wired back.

Then came this reply: "Story of creation of world told in 600. Try it."

Business

117.   An executive who is a great believer in efficiency hung up a sign in her office one day last week. It read: "Do it now."

Within 24 hours, the cashier bolted with the contents of the safe, her secretary eloped with her eldest son, the office boy threw the ink bottle into the electric fan, and the whole office force took the afternoon off.

118. A man walked into a dress shop and asked the proprietor how business was.

"Terrible!" he complained. "It's so bad, why I only sold one dress yesterday. And today it's even worse."

"How could it be worse?" asked his friend.

"Today she returned the dress she bought yesterday," wailed the proprietor.

119. A candy store operator was bemoaning the sad fate that had overtaken him. "I was a hard-working clerk, earning a meager weekly salary," he told his pastor, "when, like so many ill-advised young people, I fell in with shady characters and felt compelled to gamble."

"Ah," sympathized the minister, "and the temptation cost you all your hard-accumulated savings!"

"No," said the man. "I won—and in a moment of weakness bought this lousy candy store."

120. New York City businessperson, Norman A. Brodsky, characterizes fast business growth and creative financing with this story: A guy goes to the horse track, puts down $2 on the first race, and wins. He bets the pile on the second and wins again. He risks that on the third, and so on. Eventually, he's ahead $800,000 and—what the heck—lets everything ride on the last race. The horse finishes out of the money. When the man gets home, his wife asks how he fared. "I lost $2," he confides.

121. A new car dealer came upon hard times. He fell so deeply in debt that his banker called him in. After a long, heated visit, the car dealer inquired, "Have you ever been in the car business?"

"No, I can't say I have," said the banker.

"Well," said the distressed dealer, "you are now."

122. An American and Soviet businessperson were discussing who had more input into the operation of their company. The American said, "I can go to my boss anytime and say, 'I think there are some changes that can be made to make this company more profitable.'"

The Soviet responded, "Well, I can do that too. I can walk into the President's office anytime and say, 'Mr. President, I think there are changes Americans can make to make their companies more profitable.'"

123.   Implementing new ideas in today's corporate world is like mating elephants; it's done at a real high level and there's a lot of bellowing.

124.   "You are the glimmer of hope America needs," began a management consultant addressing high-level executives. "However, America's business culture needs to address two troubling issues. They are low employee commitment and a vision for the future. The absence of these two qualities stand out like two sumo wrestlers at a beauty contest."

C

Card-playing. See also Gambling

125. Looks are sometimes deceiving. The person with a vacant look may have a full house.

126. The police stopped a man going down the street clad in a barrel.

"Are you a poker player?" he asked.

"No," the man replied, "but I just left some people who are."

127. The zoo keeper received an indignant complaint that the monkeys were playing poker and a warning that he should do something about it right away.

"That's all right," he soothed. "They're only playing for peanuts."

128. At 3:00 A.M., the cautious husband silently inserted his key in the front door, but his wife was on hand to greet him.

"Hah!" she cried. "Three o'clock! I suppose you're going to tell me you've been out somewhere holding a sick friend's hand."

"Well," said the man sadly, "if I had been holding *his* hand, we'd be a lot richer tonight!"

129. Three patients in a hospital ward were reprimanded severely for playing poker. As a final gesture, the nurse confiscated the deck of cards.

Later, one of the patients went down the floor and collected the medical charts from the beds. He returned, shuffled the charts, and dealt them out. "I've got a pair," he said, laying down two appendectomies.

"I've got that beat," replied the second patient, showing a full house—tonsillectomies over fractured legs.

The third patient chuckled softly. "It looks like I win," he said. "I've got a royal flush." He laid down his charts—five enemas.

130. An American tourist home from Formosa told how one night he decided to kill a little time playing poker with three wealthy Chinese. As he spoke no Chinese, and they no English, they got an interpreter. All went quietly for a while, but in due course the American was dealt a four-card flush and bet a hundred dollars.

At this, the Chinese card player next to him exclaimed, "Ah moy," which the interpreter explained meant he raised a hundred. The next Chinese announced, "Ah foy," and the interpreter said, "He raises you two hundred more." The third Chinese grunted, "Ah goy," which the interpreter explained as another hundred raise.

In spite of the competition the American decided to stay with the pot, and drew his one card. Noting that he had failed to fill his flush, he cried, "Ah phooey," at which the Chinese all threw down their hands.

"Nice going, mister," cried the interpreter, slapping him on the back. "Your million dollar bluff won the pot."

Career

131. Hundreds of college freshman were attending a regional career exploration day at a local university. The students were encouraged to visit with professionals representing a variety of possible disciplines. A career counselor noticed one of her students visiting solely with a funeral home director representative.

Questioned later as to why she limited her visits to one person, the girl confidently responded, "I have known all my life that someday I would be a mortician."

"And why is that?" the counselor asked. "Because," the girl replied, "I love to work with people."

Cause and effect

132.   Two senators were lamenting the death of a colleague who had passed on the day before. "I understand," observed one, "that our friend T—left very few effects."

"It would not be otherwise," replied her friend. "He had very few causes."

Chauvinism

133.   An American staying in a London hotel was introduced to a man from Edinburgh who asked him, "An' what country do you belong tae?"

"The greatest country in the world!" replied the American.

"Mon! So dae I," replied Sandy, "but you dinna speak like a Scotsman."

134.   An aged woman, born and nurtured in the South, was endeavoring to impress upon her nephews and nieces the beauties of the South and its people, when one of the young men spoke up.

"Auntie," he asked, "do you think that all of the virtues originated and have been preserved by the Southern people?"

"No, not all, but most of them," she replied.

"Do you think that Jesus Christ was a Southerner?" asked the young man.

The elderly lady hesitated a moment and then said: "He was good enough to be a Southerner!"

Children

135.   A young mother was preparing a breakfast of ham, eggs, and toast for her daughter's slumber party friends. One of the little girls began talking about breakfast at her house. "My mom always makes us pancakes for breakfast," said the youngster.

The mother, wanting to please her daughter's friends, quickly mixed up pancake batter. When offering a short stack of hot cakes to the little girl, she responded, "No, thank you."

"But I thought your mother always made pancakes for you," the surprised mother responded.

"Oh, she does," said the girl, "but I don't eat them at home either."

136. During an open house at the school, little Jenny began talking to one of her classmates.

"Who is that little boy?" her mother asked.

"Tommy."

"What is Tommy's whole name?"

"Well, the teacher calls him Tommy Sitdown."

Child training

137. Never slap a child in the face. It is well to remember that there is a place for everything.

138. "My teenage son obeys me perfectly."

"Amazing. How do you do it?"

"I tell him to do as he pleases."

139. An elderly gentleman strolling through a quiet residential neighborhood came upon a little boy sitting on the curb crying copiously. "What's the trouble, son?" he asked. "Are you lost?"

"Worse than that," the youngster sobbed. "Mom's book on child-raising is lost, and now she's using her own judgment!"

Church affiliation

140. A business executive was interviewing a job applicant. "Now then," he stated briskly, "for this position we need a real live wire. But, at the same time, the person must be methodical. I can't overemphasize the importance of being methodical."

"Hm'm," the applicant said, after some thought, "if that's the case, I guess I don't want the job after all."

"No? Why not?"

"Well," replied the applicant, "it's that 'methodical.' All my life I've been a good Presbyterian, and I don't believe that I'm going to change now."

Church attendance

141. If people cared what other people wear, they'd be in church oftener.

142. If ever I build a church I will put this sign on every door: "You are not too bad to come in. You are not too good to stay out."

143. "Dad, can I ask you a question?"
"Sure, son."
"When am I going to be old enough not to have to go to church either?"

144. A stranger stepping into an open church for a few minutes of contemplation found a purse in the pew in front of him. Since no one else was in the church, a question promptly rose in his mind: Was this a temptation of the Devil, or the answer to a prayer?

145. A man came home and saw his children on the front steps and asked what they were doing. "We're playing church," they answered.
The puzzled father inquired further and was told, "Well, we've already sung, prayed and preached, and now we're outside on the steps smoking."

146. The chairperson for the church's Evangelism Committee was concerned about sparse attendance. In an effort to make a point and assist the pastor she published this item in the church bulletin: "This . . . is . . . the . . . way . . . the . . . church . . . sometimes . . . looks . . . to . . . the . . . pastor . . . when . . . he . . . goes . . . into . . . the . . . pulpit.
"Wouldlooklikethisifeverybodybroughtsomebodyelseto-church."

147. At a mental hospital in California one Sunday morning a group of patients were being shepherded to the Catholic and Protestant chapels. One patient did not enter either chapel, but continued walking toward the main gate. When an attendant caught up with him and asked where he was going the patient replied, "I was told I could go to the church of my choice, and that is in New York."

148. The little boy was late for Sunday school, and the superintendent, seeing him slip in, detained him and asked him the reason. The boy shuffled his feet uncertainly for a moment, then blurted out: "I started out to go fishing instead, but my dad wouldn't let me."

The superintendent beamed broadly. "A wise father," he said. "He was quite right not to let you go fishing on a Sunday. Did he explain to you why?"

The little boy nodded. "Oh, yes, sir. He said there wasn't enough bait for the two of us."

Church collections

149. "I've been racking my brains, but I can't place you," one man said to another at a gathering. "And you look very much like somebody I have seen a lot—somebody I don't like but I can't tell you why. Isn't that strange?"

"Nothing strange about it," the other man said. "You have seen me a lot and I know why you resent me. For two years I passed the collection plate in your church."

150. Little Mary was much surprised when she received a half dollar on her fifth birthday. She kept it in her hands constantly, and finally sat down on a stool, looking intently at the coin.

Her mother said, "Mary, what are you going to do with your half dollar?"

"I'll take it with me to Sunday school," said Mary promptly.

"I guess you want to show it to your teacher," suggested mother.

"Oh, no!" declared Mary. "I'm going to give it to God. I know He will be as surprised as I am to get something besides pennies!"

Citizenship

151. A Frenchman renounced his citizenship to become a British subject. "What have you gained by it?" demanded a countryman.

"Well," said the former Frenchman, "for one thing, I have now won the Battle of Waterloo."

152.   A refugee couple arrived in the United States several years ago with one dream—to become citizens. Through much red tape and years of study, they were patient and hopeful. Then one day, the husband rushed into the kitchen with the long-awaited good news.

"Anna! Anna!" he shouted. "At last! We are Americans!"

"Fine," replied the wife, tying her apron around him. "Now you wash the dishes."

Civilization

153.   An explorer came across a native village in the jungle. "You people are lost to civilization," he observed to the chief.

"We don't mind being lost," was the reply. "It's being discovered that worries us."

Clergy

154.   A small country preacher, a television evangelist, and a mutual friend were in a boat 25 yards from shore. The preacher stepped out and nonchalantly walked to land. The evangelist duplicated the exit on the water. Then the friend stepped out and sank. Coming up, he got back in the boat, walked out, and went under again.

The preacher and evangelist stood on the shore watching their friend's futile attempts. Finally, the preacher dryly said to the evangelist, "Do you think we should tell him where the rocks are?"

155.   Bishop Fulton J. Sheen was scheduled to speak one evening at the town hall in Philadelphia. Although unfamiliar with the city, Sheen decided to walk from his hotel and enjoy the sights along the way. Unfortunately, he became lost and had no idea which direction to turn. Approaching a group of 'street wise' boys, Bishop Sheen asked directions to his destination. One of the boys asked Sheen what he was going to do at the town hall. "I'm going to give a lecture," replied the Bishop. "About what?" "On how to get to heaven. Would you like to come along?" "Are you kidding?" said the boy, "you don't even know how to get to the town hall!"

Class reunion. See Reunion, Class

Club Membership

156. On being invited to join an actors' club, Groucho Marx remarked: "I wouldn't belong to any organization that would have me for a member."

157. "I've got too many organization dues to pay," Mrs. Hillis murmured over her checkbook. "One of these days somebody's going to read on my tombstone—'Christine Hillis. Clubbed to death.'"

158. "I am the recording secretary of a chess club," the man advised the judge who had asked him for his occupation.
"And what are your duties?"
"I read the hours of the last meeting."

Coexistence

159. Zoo visitors were amazed to see a cage, labeled "Coexistence," containing a lion and some lambs.
The zoo director explained there was nothing to it. "Just add a few fresh lambs every now and then."

College

160. The type of education a college person gets sometimes depends on the type of institution he attends—educational or coeducational.

161. "The college I went to turned out some great people."
"When did you graduate?"
"I didn't exactly graduate. I was turned out."

162. *Friend:* "Has your son's college education proved helpful since you took him into the firm?"

Father: "Oh yes, whenever we have a conference, we let him mix the cocktails."

163. *Friend:* "You look all broken up."
College student: "I wrote home for money for a study lamp."
Friend: "So what?"
College student: "They sent the lamp."

164. "How come your son is doing so well in college?"
"Well, wine makes him sick, he's afraid of women, he hates to play games, he's allergic to the sun, and he can't sing, so he just stays home and studies."

Common cause

165. "Some years ago I was driving down Broadway with my sister. Suddenly she boomed out, 'Slow up. Slow up. Slow up.' I don't know why, but somehow women always say things three times.

"Just to show her who was driving the car, I said, Shut up, and for emphasis pressed my foot on the accelerator. We really started to move down Broadway. But not for long.

"Out of nowhere came a gorilla on a motorcyle. A siren screeched—and a roar deafened my ears—'GET OVER THERE!' The car whimpered to the curb automatically.

"After what seemed eternity a huge head filled the whole window of the car.

" 'What's the hurry?' he rasped.

"There didn't seem any hurry at that point—but just then my mother's favorite daughter howled, 'Give him a ticket, Officer. Give him a ticket. He's always speeding, always, always.'

" 'Get out of that car, Bud,' panted the Gorilla.

"I walked to the rear of the car, thinking, 'I'll get thirty days for this one!'

"As I looked up at the towering policeman he leaned down over me and in the softest voice you ever heard whispered, '*Go on, Bud, I got one at home just like her.*' "

David Guy Powers

Communication

166.   Several years ago, a seasoned plumber wrote to the U.S. Bureau of Standards promoting a new procedure for cleaning pipes. The bureau replied: "The efficiency of the recommended solution is completely undisputed. However, there is an inherent incompatibility between the aforementioned solution and the basic chemical structures of the commonly used materials in current household and commercial pipeworks."

The plumber wrote back saying, "Thanks, I really liked it, too."

Within a few days, the Bureau responded with another letter: "Don't use hydrochloric acid! It eats holes in pipes!"

Communism

167.   A famous athlete, who had recently escaped from behind the Iron Curtain, was asked why the Russians excelled in marathon running.

He replied: "We use the border for the finish line."

168.   A German and a Russian were fishing on opposite sides of the river. The German caught fish after fish, while the Russian didn't even get a bite. Finally the Russian yelled across, "Why is it you catch fish and I get none?"

The German thought a minute and then replied, "I guess on your side they are afraid to open their mouths."

169.   Three cellmates in a Soviet hoosegow compared notes.

"I was jailed for coming late to work," mourned the first.

"Me? I came too early," recounted the second. "They said this proved I was a Capitalist spy."

"And I'm here," complained the third, "because I arrived exactly on time. They accused me of owning an American watch."

170.   A French poodle met a Russian wolfhound on the Champs Elysees in Paris. "How are things in Russia?" asked the French poodle.

"Fabulous," the Russian wolfhound replied. "I sleep in a solid gold dog house on a sable carpet, and all day long they feed me caviar."

"Well," asked the French poodle, "if things are so good in Russia, why do you come to Paris?" The Russian wolfhound leaned forward. "Well," he whispered confidentially, "sometimes I like to bark."

171. A Moscow father was complimenting another on his three sons.

"You must be mighty proud of them," he said. "One a people's doctor, one a people's lawyer, and one a people's artist."

"Yes, they're fine boys," said the father, "but the son I'm really proud of is in America."

"Oh, he's an American?"

"Yes, indeed—he's unemployed and gets money from the government and if it weren't for the few dollars he sends home we'd starve."

172. A small Russian boy was asked by his teacher, "What is the size of the Communist Party?"

"About five feet two inches," he promptly replied.

"No, no!" exploded the teacher. "I mean how many members does it have? How do you get five feet two inches?"

"Well," replied the boy, "my father is six feet tall and every night he puts his hand to his chin and says, 'I've *had* the Communist Party, up to here!'"

173. In a Warsaw schoolroom, little Janek was asked to give an example of a dependent clause.

"Our cat has a litter of ten kittens," he piped, "all of which are good Communists."

Teacher, delighted with his grasp of grammar and Party Line, urged him to do as well when the government inspector made his annual visit.

Next week, with the inspector sternly observing, teacher confidently called on Janek.

"Our cat has a litter of ten kittens," Janek piped, "all of which are good Western Democrats."

Teacher cried, "Why, Janek! That is not what you said a week ago."

"Yes," replied Janek very seriously, "but my kittens' eyes are open now."

174.   There was a meeting in an iron curtain country at which one of the party members, Comrade Popsky, got up and said, "Comrade leader, I have only three questions to ask. If we are the greatest industrial nation in the world, what happened to our automobiles? If we have the best agriculture in the world, what happened to our bread? If we are the finest cattle raisers in the world, what happened to our meat?"

The presiding chair stared at Comrade Popsky, hardly believing what he heard. Then he answered, "It is too late to reply to your questions tonight. At our next meeting I will answer them fully."

When the meeting opened the following week, another party member rose and said, "I have just one question. What happened to Comrade Popsky?"

Competition

175.   A bunch of chickens was in the yard when a football flew over the fence and landed in their midst. A rooster waddled over, studied it, then said: "I'm not complaining, girls, but look at the work they're turning out next door."

176.   Competition can be compared to the two hikers who spotted a mountain lion stalking them. One of the hikers calmly sat down, took off his hiking boots, and began putting on his running shoes. "What good are those shoes going to do you?" asked his buddy. "You can't outrun a mountain lion!" Lacing up his tennies, the friend responded, "I don't have to outrun the lion. I figure staying ahead of you will do just fine."

Complaint—Complaints

177.   One stormy night, Frank Lloyd Wright, noted Wisconsin architect, was roused from a sound sleep by an urgent phone call from a client who had just moved into his Wright-built house.

"There's a leak in the roof and the living room is flooded," cried the man. "What shall I do?"

Advised Wright, "Rise above it."

178.   The desk clerk received a call from one of the hotel's guests, an elderly single woman, who complained, "There's a man across the court taking a shower and he's got the blinds up."

The house detective was sent to the woman's room to investigate. He looked out her window and then said, "I can't see a man over there."

"You can't?" replied the old maid. "Get up on that trunk and look again."

179.   A young man joined a monastery which required recruits to abide by strict behavior guidelines. Each person took a vow of silence with the understanding they could speak two words a year with their superior. At the end of the first year, the young man was called by his superior to make his first two-word statement. He said, "room smells." Another year passed and he got his second chance. His next two words were "food bad." At the end of the third year, he approached his superior with clenched fists, tension-filled face, and with a shout said, "I quit!" The superior remained calm and responded, "I'm not surprised. All you have done since you got here is complain, complain, complain."

Conceit

180.   Sir Herbert Beerbohm Tree, British actor and manager, once berated a young actor for his overbearing conceit.

"I assure you, sir," said the other indignantly, "that I am not suffering from a swelled head."

"It isn't the swelling that causes suffering," retorted Tree. "It's the subsequent shrinkage that hurts."

181.   A man who thought highly of himself stepped on a coin-operated scale that voiced his calculated weight. The high-tech machine then dispensed a card with comments about his personality. He read the card and with a broad smile covering his face, handed it to his friend. "Here, read this!" She took it and read aloud, "You are a well-built, enthusiastic, dynamic leader, admired by your peers." In disbelief, she read it once again and commented, "Just remember, the machine had your weight wrong too."

Confusion

182.   It seems to me that we're all in the same boat with Christopher Columbus. He didn't know where he was going when he started. When he got there he didn't know where he was, and when he got back he didn't know where he had been.

183.   The biology club at the university was sponsored by one of the professors, a dignified lady who had chosen to remain single. A farmer, whose place was noted for its wide variety of flowers, spoke at one of the meetings.

More at home in his garden than as a speaker, he began by saying, "I can assure you that it is a pleasure for me to be with you today. I have known your teacher a good many years and during that time we have been intimate."

There was a slight titter and he hastily continued, "in a biological sense, of course."

Conscience

184.   An eager-beaver salesperson was trying to have a country storekeeper carry his product, and finally tried to bribe the fellow with a bottle of champagne.

"Oh, my conscience wouldn't let me take a gift," the business owner protested.

"What if I sell it to you for a dime?" asked the salesperson.

"In that case," replied the man, "I'll take two."

Consultants

185.   A management consultant died and went to meet her maker. As she approached the pearly gates, she noticed beautiful gold streamers, a large, pure-white cake, an orchestra playing, and thousands of angels singing. St. Peter rushed over to shake the lawyer's hand. "I've never seen such a celebration," said the new arrival.

"Well, you're very special," St. Peter explained. "We've never had anyone live to be 120 before."

The consultant was puzzled. "But I'm only 59."

St. Peter thought for a moment. "Oh," he said, "we must have added up your billing hours."

Context, Out of

186. A sedate English literary man was interviewed by reporters on his arrival in New York. He remembered that he had been warned before leaving London that American newshawks would probably try to make a fool of him.

"Are you going to visit any night clubs during your stay in New York?" was the first question asked.

"Are there any night clubs in New York?" parried the literary man.

The next day he opened his morning paper to an account of the interview. According to the story, the first question he had asked on stepping ashore was: "Are there any night clubs in New York?"

Conversation

187. Three ways to break up a dinner conversation . . .

1. Ask the person on your right if he or she is married. If they say yes, ask if he or she has any children. If they say no, ask him or her how they do it.

2. Ask the person on your left if they are married. If they say no, ask if they have any children.

3. Lean across the table and ask the person facing you if they have any children. If they say yes, ask if they are married.

Cooking

188. "Jack, wake up. There's a burglar in the kitchen and he's eating up the rest of the pie we had for dinner."

"Go back to sleep. I'll bury him in the morning."

189. "I clipped this recipe from a magazine in the reading room of the library," said the cook. "I suppose I did wrong."

Mother, *surveying the dish:* "You undoubtedly incurred the wrath of the librarians, but on the other hand, no one knows how many families ought to be eternally grateful."

190.　It was baking day and mother was being assisted by her ten-year-old daughter.

"Paula," she said, "open the oven and see if that coffee cake is baked. Just stick in a knife and see if it comes out clean."

Paula returned in a few minutes and said, "Mom, the knife came out so clean I stuck in all the other dirty knives."

191.　A young bride had not come out very well in her first encounter with the cook book and gas stove. She ran to the telephone and called her mother.

"Mother," she sobbed, "I can't understand it. The recipe says clearly, 'bring to a boil on brisk fire, stirring for two minutes. Then beat it for ten minutes.' And when I came back again, it was burned to a cinder."

Cooperation

192.　There is little chance for people to get together as long as most of us want to be in the front of the bus, the back of the church, and the middle of the road.

Courage

193.　"I resent your remark," said the fifth grader. "And I'll give you just five seconds to take it back!"

"Oh, yeah," snarled the seventh grader. "Suppose I don't take it back in five seconds?"

"Well," said the first, "how much time do you want?"

194.　Having missed his train to the suburbs a meek young man decided to fortify himself with a drink or two. Finding the liquor a great consolation he started back to the station, but lost his way. While groping about he happened to pass a zoo, and feeling sleepy, he opened the lion's cage and fell asleep with his head comfortably resting on the king of beasts' stomach.

The next day his wife set out to search for him and found him snoring blissfully in the middle of the lion's den. "Come out of there," she shrieked. "Come out, you little coward!"

195. Dr. Charles Garfield, author of *Peak Performance,* tells the story of a very wealthy man who bought a huge ranch in Arizona and invited some of his closest associates in to see it. After touring some of the 1500 acres of mountains and rivers and grasslands, he took everybody to the house. The house was as spectacular as the scenery, and out back was the largest swimming pool you have ever seen. However, this gigantic swimming pool was filled with alligators. The rich owner explained this way: "I value courage more than anything else. Courage is what made me a billionaire. In fact, I think that courage is such a powerful virtue that if anybody is courageous enough to jump in that pool, swim through those alligators and make it to the other side, I'll give them anything they want, anything—my house, my land, my money." Of course, everybody laughed at the absurd challenge and proceeded to follow the owner into the house for lunch . . . when they suddenly heard a splash. Turning around they saw this guy swimming for his life across the pool, thrashing at the water, as the alligators swarmed after him. After several death-defying seconds, the man made it, unharmed to the other side. Our rich host was absolutely amazed, but he stuck to his promise. He said, "You are indeed a man of courage and I will stick to my word. What do you want? You can have anything—my house, my land, my money—just tell me what you want and it is yours." The swimmer, breathing heavily, looked up at the host and said, "I just want to know one thing—who the hell pushed me into that pool?"!

Courtship. See also Romance

196. *He:* "Have you ever loved before?"
She: "No, John. I've often admired men for their looks, strength, courage, intelligence, or something like that. But with you, John, it's love—nothing else."

Cowardice

197. "I'd like to make an appointment with the dentist please."

"Sorry, he's out just now."
"When will he be out again?"

198.   A tough governor's race resulted in the incumbent disposing of a tough opponent with this gem of political destruction: "My opponent brags that he is a hard-boiled egg! Well, folks, I never saw a hard-boiled egg that didn't have a yellow heart!"

Credit

199.   "Do you live within your income?"
"Certainly not. I have all I can do to live within my credit."

200.   An elderly farmer wrote to a mail order house as follows: "Please send me one of the gasoline engines you show on page 787, and if it's any good, I'll send you a check."

In time he received the following reply: "Please send check. If it's any good, we'll send the engine."

201.   When a familiar face was missing from the regular get-togethers the wife of one of the social group called to inquire the reason.

"You might as well know the truth," the man's wife said. "I put so much pressure on Bob to keep up appearances that he went out and got two years for stealing a Cadillac."

When Bob was paroled a few months later the couple found themselves ostracized by their old crowd; the woman who had called explained the reason.

"We can't mingle with criminals," she said bluntly. "Why did you have to steal a Cadillac? Couldn't you buy one and not pay for it, like the rest of us?"

Credulity

202.   A group of foreign manufacturers, who were being shown through an American plant, saw a machine that took a piece of sheet steel and in one operation stamped, punched, and shaped it into a finished product. After they had watched it for a time, an apparently bitter argument broke out among them, with much arm-waving and finger-shaking. The guide asked the interpreter accompanying the party what all the shouting was about.

"Some of them," replied the interpreter nonchalantly, "insist it can't be done!"

Crime—Punishment

203.   A teacher asked the class to name some of the benefits of the automotive age. After a silence, one boy spoke up, "Well, it stopped horse stealing."

Criticism

204.   It's better to help others get on than to tell them where to get off.

205.   A prominent New York Theater Critic was leaving the theater after a Broadway opening and met the producer in the lobby. The latter took one look at the critic's suit, which was rumpled as usual, and said with some annoyance:

"That's a fine way to dress for my opening. Your suit looks as if it had been slept in."

"Since you mention it," he replied, "I just woke up."

Customer Service

206.   A high school student landed her first summer job working in a drugstore. As she arrived at the store for her first day on the job, the phone was ringing. Everyone was busy and the manager asked her to please answer the phone.

"Good morning," she said in a cheery voice.

"Do you stock Ben Gay?" queried the caller.

"I'm not sure."

"Well, does your store carry Vicks Vap-O-Rub?"

"I don't know."

"Do you have Pepto-Bismol on hand?"

"I couldn't tell you for sure if we do or don't."

"You don't know much do you, young lady," said the caller.

"No, I guess I don't," the young lady responded. "In fact, when I said 'good morning,' I told you everything I know."

207.   An impatient airline customer was giving the luggage checker at the Minneapolis Airport a difficult time. There seemed to be something wrong with everything the employee said or did.

CUSTOMER SERVICE   **47**

Another customer, waiting in line, observed the abuse the young man was enduring. When his turn came, the man commented that this must be a thankless job, especially having to put up with the comments of critical people.

"Oh, you must be referring to that last guy," the checker responded. "It's alright, I've already gotten even with him!"

"What do you mean?" asked the concerned flyer.

"Well, he's all set to go to Philadelphia," said the young man. "But his luggage is on the way to San Francisco."

208. An electric company used a unique approach to collect overdue bills. After 30 days, they sent a letter which simply said: "We would be delighted if you would promptly pay your bill. However, you'll be de-lighted if you don't."

209. Comedy writer Bob Orben comments on customer service: "I love it. You go to a coin-operated store to wash and dry your clothes. Then you go to a filling station where you pump your own gas. And on to a fast food restaurant where you carry your own tray. And what is it being called? A service economy!"

210. Returning change to a customer, the sales clerk mumbled something. "I'm sorry," said the customer, "I didn't hear what you said."

"I said have a great day," snapped the clerk. "What are you, deaf or something?"

211. After-Christmas complaints and returns flooded the department store. One customer service person patiently listened to a disgruntled customer complaining non-stop about an item she had purchased. Unable to get a word in edgewise, the service representative finally interrupted with: "I'm sorry for the inconvenience we have caused you. If I were to refund your money, give you a free replacement, and then commit suicide, would that be helpful?"

212. The story is told of a flower shop in a large mall crowded with customers waiting for attention. The phone rang at the check-out counter and the caller ordered a dozen long-stem roses. The sales clerk asked where the flowers should be delivered.

"Don't bother sending them," said the customer. "Just bring them to the counter. I'm calling from a pay phone outside your store."

213. Several years ago, a Blondie cartoon pictured Dagwood complaining to the cook that the chicken croquettes he had been served were too small. After tasting one, he added, "and they taste horrible." The quick-thinking server responded, "Then you're lucky they are small."

214. Sign in a department store's Customer Service Department:
"God Loves You And I'm Trying"

D

Dancing

215. It happened in a teenage rock-n-roll joint. The waiter dropped a tray of dishes and six couples got up to dance.

Debt

216. *Ted:* "I started out on the theory that the world had an opening for me."
Fred: "And you found it?"
Ted: "Well, kinda, I'm in the hole now."

217. *Sympathizer:* "Tell me, friend, how did you ever get yourself into such destitute circumstances?"
Depressed Man: "Well, when I had the world by the tail, I let go to reach for the moon."

Debtor—Creditor

218. Running into debt isn't so bad. It's running into creditors that hurts.

219. The installment collector came around to remind Joe he was seven payments behind on his piano. "Well," replied Joe, "the company advertises 'pay as you play'—and I play very poorly."

220. "I don't see why you haggled so with the tailor about the price—you'll never pay his bill, anyhow," said Pat to Mike.
"Yes, but, you see, I'm conscientious. I don't want the poor fellow to lose more than is necessary."

221. The butcher confronted the customer with embarrassment. "I'm sorry, madam, but I can't give you further credit. Your bill is bigger now than it should be."

"I'm aware of that," the woman exclaimed. "If you'll make it out for what it should be, I'll pay it."

222. "Will you tell me, my dear friend, how you manage, that you are never pressed for money, but always have plenty of it?"

"That is very simple; I never pay old debts."

"But how about the new ones?"

"I let them grow old."

223. A taxpayer received a strongly worded "second notice" that his taxes were overdue. Hastening to the collector's office, he paid his bill, saying apologetically that he had overlooked the first notice.

"Oh," confided the collector with a smile, "we don't send out first notices. We have found that the second notices are more effective."

224. A merchant tried for many months to collect an overdue bill, but with no success. Finally, he sent a tear-jerking letter accompanied by a picture of his little daughter. Under it he wrote, "The reason I need the money."

By return mail came a photo of a family with six children. It was captioned, "The reason I can't pay."

225. A man called a dozen of his creditors to tell them that he was about to go into bankruptcy.

"I owe you over $100,000," he said, "and my assets aren't enough to pay you five cents on the dollar. So I guess it will be impossible for you to get anything—unless you want to cut me up and divide me among you."

"Say, Mr. president," spoke up one creditor, "I move we do it. I'd like to have his gall."

226. In one of those familiar, old western scenes on TV, two groups of men were shooting it out in the barroom of a shabby roadhouse.

Suddenly a meek little man entered the door and started right across the room toward the bar. All the shooting stopped.

The bartender got up from behind the safety of the bar and said, "Partner, it sure took real courage to walk right through all those six guns without lookin' right nor left."

"Not at all," replied the meek little man as he asked for a sarsaparilla. "You see, I owe money to every one in the place."

Deception

227.   Two little fellows coming home from Sunday school were discussing the lesson.

"Say, do you believe all that about the devil?"

"No, don't let them kid you. That's just like Santa Claus—it's your dad."

Decisions

228.   Comedian Jack Benny, during one of his acts, was confronted by an armed robber who said, "Your money or your life." The demand was followed by ten seconds of silence. Then, just as the audience expected a reply, Benny pondered the demand again.

Finally, the robber repeated: "Hey mister, what will it be, your money or your life?"

Benny calmly replied: "I'm thinking. I'm thinking."

229.   "When you come to a fork in the road, take it."
                                                    Yogi Berra

230.   Most people do not enjoy making decisions. They're like the confused young man who went to a psychiatrist. The psychiatrist empathetically listened to his patient and then offered his insight. "It appears to me you have trouble making decisions. Would you agree?" The young man pondered for a moment, and then responded, "Well, yes and no."

Democracy

231.   The hydrogen bomb has made one great contribution to democracy. With it—all men are cremated equal.

Destination

232.   The average person's life consists of twenty years of having parents ask where they are going; forty years of having a spouse ask the same question; and at the end, the mourners wondering, too.

233.   A man "butted in" at a waiting line before the ticket window in New York and the people who were in a hurry glowered.

"I want a ticket for Boston," said the man, and he put a dollar under the wicket.

"You can't go to Boston for a dollar," returned the ticket agent.

"Well, then," asked the man, "where can I go for a dollar?"

And each of the fourteen men in that waiting line quickly told him!

Determination

234.   A young college graduate, determined to find a position with a reputable company, began seeking interviews. Although she faced continual rejection, this persevering talent kept her goals in mind. One busy personnel manager, flooded with applications, suggested the hopeful applicant check back in ten years. "No problem," the young woman responded. "Would a morning or afternoon interview work best for you?"

Diagnosis

235.   The middle-aged man was shuffling along, bent over at the waist, as his wife helped him into the doctor's waiting room. A woman in the office viewed the scene in sympathy. "Arthritis with complications?" she asked.

The wife shook her head. "Do-it-yourself," she explained, "with concrete blocks."

236.   Being human, doctors are reluctant to make appointments where receipt of payment is doubtful. Under these circumstances a physician diagnosed a patient's illness on the phone. "There is nothing wrong with your uncle. I have examined him thoroughly and I tell you he only thinks he's sick. He thinks he's sick."

A week later the doctor met the patient's nephew. "How's your uncle?" he asked.

"Worse," said the relative. "Now he thinks he's dead."

Diet—Dieting

237.　Diets are for people who are thick and tired of it.

238.　Seating his dinner guests, a doctor asked, "Are we going to eat like people or animals?" The somewhat shocked guests replied: "Like people, of course."

"Oh, that's too bad," said the doctor, "because animals would stop eating when they got enough."

239.　Methuselah ate what he found on his plate,
And never, as people do now,
Did he note the amount of the calorie count;
He ate it because it was chow.

He wasn't disturbed as at dinner he sat,
Devouring a roast or a pie,
To think it was lacking in granular fat
Or a couple of vitamins shy.

He cheerfully chewed each species of food,
Unmindful of troubles or fears
Lest his health might be hurt
By some fancy dessert;
And he lived over 900 years.

Author unknown

240.　"I'm on such a strict diet," the woman lamented, "I can't even listen to dinner music."

241.　"I think we can get your weight under control," said the doctor confidently, "if we can just overcome the Noah problem."

"What do you mean?" questioned the overweight patient.

"Every time you sit down to eat," advised the doctor, "stop taking two of everything."

242.   Did you read about the man who went on a powdered food diet. It was working quite well until he went out in the rain . . . and immediately gained 22 pounds.

243.   From "The Fat Man's Prayer" by Victor Buono comes this solemn thought: "We are what we eat," said the wise old man, "and Lord if that's true, then I'm a garbage can."

244.   "Lord, if you can't make me thin, then make my friends look fat."

Erma Bombeck

245.   Out of the annals of present-day diet mania comes the story of a woman attempting to stick to a "no sweets" menu. Unfortunately, visions of desserts, candy and other sugar-filled food dances through her mind.

"Think about things that make you sick," her doctor suggested. "In that way you will get your mind off the desired sweets."

For awhile the doctor's suggestion worked. Then one day, the craving for sweets became overwhelming. The woman tried thinking about bugs. As she concentrated, thoughts of two boll-weevils crept into her mind. On the back of the largest insect were the words: hot fudge sundae. On the back of the smaller bug were the words: chocolate mint. The woman couldn't resist any longer. She broke down and ate the chocolate mint. It was the lesser of two weevils.

246.   Joe's idea of a low-calorie diet is a martini without the olive.

247.   From the *Optimist* magazine comes a new approach to dieting. It's called the pasta diet. Just walk pasta bakery without stopping. Walk pasta candy store without stopping. Walk pasta ice cream shop without stopping . . .

248.   Diet tips:
1. If no one sees you eat it, it has no calories.
2. If you drink a diet soda with a candy bar, they cancel each other out.

3. When eating with someone else, calories don't count if you both eat the same amount.

4. Food used for medicinal purposes NEVER counts, such as hot chocolate, brandy, toast, and Sara Lee cheesecake.

5. If you fatten up everyone else around you, you look thinner.

6. Movie-related foods don't count because they are simply part of the entertainment experience and not a part of one's personal fuel, such as Milk Duds, popcorn with butter, and Junior Mints.

Enjoy Your Diet!!!!!

Source Unknown

Difference—Differences

249.   The difference between a mistress and a wife is the difference between day and night.

250.   A celebrated judge and an almost equally celebrated bishop were engaged in friendly argument as to which of them had more power over the human race. Explained the bishop: "After all, old man, you can only say to a person, 'You be hanged! I can go very much further. I can say to a person, 'You be damned!'"

The judge nodded, smilingly. "Ah, yes," he said. "But the difference is that when I say to someone 'You be hanged!'—they are hanged."

251.   Adolf Hitler was very much disturbed when a clairvoyant let it be known that she could predict the exact day of the Fuhrer's death. Since her predictions were always based on astrology, and since Hitler himself was a believer in the stars, he sent for the woman. After much divination the woman finally said that the omens indicated no specific date for the passing of the Nazi leader, other than that it would definitely take place on a Jewish holiday.

"Which holiday?" Hitler demanded.

"I cannot be sure," said the astrologist.

"You've got to be sure," Hitler ordered, going off into one of his spastic shrieks. "I demand that you be sure."

"What difference does it make?" shrugged the woman. "Any day on which you die will be a Jewish holiday."

Dilemma

252.   From a small midwestern town newspaper comes this story depicting a common American dilemma.

"This fellow starts out his day early, having set his alarm clock (made in Japan) for 6 a.m. While his coffee pot (made in Japan) is perking, he puts his hair dryer (made in Taiwan) to work and shaves his face with his electric razor (made in Taiwan).

He puts on a dress shirt (made in Taiwan) and designer jeans (made in Hong Kong) with a neat pair of tennis shoes (made in Korea).

After cooking up some breakfast in his new electric skillet (made in Japan), he sits down to figure out how much he can spend this day on his calculator (made in Mexico).

After setting his watch (made in Hong Kong) to the radio (made in Japan), he goes out, gets in his car (made in Japan) and goes looking for a good-paying American job.

At the end of a disgusting day, this man decides to relax for awhile. He puts on a pair of sandals (made in Hong Kong), pours himself a glass of wine (made in France) and turns on his television (made in Japan), all this time trying to figure out why he can't find a decent job.

253.   With tears in her eyes, the little girl told her kindergarten teacher that the only coat left on the coat rack wasn't hers.

The teacher searched the rack and the classroom but she couldn't find any other coat. "Are you sure this coat isn't yours?" she asked.

"I'm sure," the little girl sobbed. "My coat had snow on it."

254.   President Harry Truman enjoyed telling the story about a man who was hit over the head on a construction site. The blow was so severe he was knocked unconscious for an extended period of time. The family, convinced he was dead, made arrangements with the funeral home to pick up the man for burial preparation. Before sun-up the next day, the man suddenly regained consciousness and sat straight up in the casket. Confused by his physical surroundings, he blinked several times and looked around. He thought: "If I'm alive, what in the world am I doing in this soft, satin-filled box? And if I'm dead, why do I have to go to the bathroom?"

255. Charles Swindoll[1] relates the unfortunate experience of four guys who decided to go mountain climbing one weekend. In the middle of the climb, one fella slipped over a cliff, dropped about sixty feet, and landed with a thud on the ledge below. The other three, hoping to rescue him, yelled, "Joe, are you okay?"

"I'm alive . . . but I think I broke both my arms!"

"We'll toss a rope down to you and pull you up. Just lie still!"

"Fine," answered Joe.

A couple of minutes after dropping one end of the rope, they started tugging and grunting together, working feverishly to pull their wounded companion to safety. When they had him about three-fourths of the way up, they suddenly remembered he said he had broken both of his arms.

"Joe! If you broke both your arms, how in the world are you hanging on?"

Joe responded, "With my TEEEEEEEEEETH . . ."

256. "I'm concerned about my husband," a woman told a therapist. "He is convinced he's a baby grand piano."

"Well, bring him in for a visit."

"I couldn't do that!" she exclaimed. "Do you know what it costs to move a piano?"

Direction—Directions

257. At a New England dog show, two elderly matrons, after looking over the various breeds asked a young attendant, "Can you direct us to the Labradors?"

"Yes ma'am," replied the boy. "Straight down this aisle, and the second door on the left."

258. An old lady kept asking the bus driver to tell her

---

[1] *Come Before Winter*, copyright 1985, Charles Swindoll, Multnomah Press, p. 195.

when they arrived at a certain small town. She asked so often that finally the driver got nervous and passed through the small town before he realized it. He apologized to the other passengers, turned around, and drove back. Then he said to the old lady: "This is the town where you wanted to get out."

"Who wants to get out?" she answered.

The driver said: "You did."

"No," she said, "my daughter told me that when I pass through this town, I should take my pills."

259. During World War I, the London clubs extended courtesies to officers of Dominion Forces, much to the annoyance of the retired field officers who were accustomed to preempt the leather armchairs in the club library. One afternoon, a colonial officer, slightly the worse for cocktails, entered the library, tapped a grumpy old general on the shoulder and asked a question using very vulgar language.

The general dropped his newspaper, screwed his monocle in his eye and looked the colonial up and down and said, "Go out that door, turn left till you come to a corridor. Follow the corridor until you come to a sign marked *gentlemen* . . . but don't let that deter you!"

Disappointment

260. The minister of a church discovered at the last minute that he hadn't invited a little old lady congregant to come to his garden party and called her up and asked her to come out.

"It's no use," she informed him. "I've already prayed for rain."

261. His team was behind one run in the ninth inning, two were out and the bases were loaded. He was the leading hitter on the team. The crowd sat on the edge of its seat as he swung two bats, threw away one, picked up the rosin bag, dropped it, straightened his cap, knocked the dirt from his spikes, wiped his brow, raised the bat over his shoulder and wiggled it, pounded it on the plate, straightened his cap once more, pulled up his pants, dug his spikes in, cocked his bat over his shoulder, reached forward—and then watched the pitcher pick the runner off third base.

Divorce

262. *Lawyer:* "Why do you want a divorce?"
Disgruntled Husband: "Because we have nothing in common. Why, we don't even hate the same people."

263. *Disillusioned wife:* "I'd like to get a divorce. My husband and I just don't get along."
Friend: "Why don't you sue on the grounds of incompatibility."
Wife: "I would if I could catch him at it."

264. A couple whose marriage was going on the rocks sought the advice of a marriage counsellor.

The counsellor pleaded with them to patch up their quarrel, but they were adamant. "So," said the counsellor, "you know the consequences and you want to part. Remember this. You must divide your property equally."

The wife flared up. "You mean the $4,000 I have saved up? I must give him half? My money?"

"Yes," said the counsellor. "He gets $2,000. You get $2,000."

"What about my furniture? I paid for that."

"Same thing," answered the counsellor. "Your husband gets the bedroom and the living room; you get the dining room and the kitchen."

There was a challenging gleam in the wife's eye. "What about our three children?"

That stumped him. Shrewdly he assayed the situation, then he came up with a Solomonic answer. "Go back and live together until your fourth child is born. Then you take two children and your husband takes two."

The wife shook her head. "No, I'm sure that wouldn't work out. If I depended on him, I wouldn't have the three I got."

Doctor—Patient

265. There's another advantage in being poor. The doctor will cure you faster.

266. "His doctor told him he was in as good shape as a man of 60, but the trouble was he was only 45."

267. "Oh, doctor," said the young lady, "will the scar show?"

"That, madam," said the doctor, "is entirely up to you."

268. *Doctor:* "Well, you are coughing with less exertion today!"

Patient: "That's not surprising, doctor, since I practiced that all night."

269. The surgeon was discussing a forthcoming operation with a wealthy patient.

"Would you prefer a local anaesthetic?" he inquired.

"I can afford the best," replied the wealthy patient. "Get something imported."

270. A town doctor was in bed when his phone rang and an excited voice told him that the baby had swallowed a corkscrew. The doctor was about to leave for the hospital emergency room when his phone rang again.

The same voice on the line said: "It's all right now, doctor. We've found another corkscrew."

271. A man living in the hill country was making his first visit to a hospital where his teenage son was about to have an operation. Watching the doctor's every move, he asked, "What's that?"

The doctor explained, "This is an anaesthetic; after he gets this he won't know a thing."

"Save your time, Doc," exclaimed the man, "he don't know anything now."

272. A contractor was hosting his friends at an open house affair to celebrate the opening of a new shop and showroom.

"If my doctor could see me with this champagne and caviar, he'd go crazy," the host confided to a friend.

"Why?" asked the buddy. "You supposed to be on a diet?"

"Naw," replied the contractor. "I owe him $300."

273. A fellow consulted a doctor because he wasn't feeling well.

"Do you smoke excessively?" asked the M.D.

"No."

"Drink a lot?"

"No."

"Keep late hours?"

"Nope."

The doctor shook his head and asked, "How can I cure you if you have nothing to give up?"

274.   Just after Pete was admitted to the hospital, he heard a knock at the door of his room. "Come in," Pete said, and in came a woman. "I'm your doctor," she said. "Please take off your clothes."

Pete asked her if she meant for him to remove all of his clothing and she told him that was just what she did mean. So he took off all his clothes and she examined him: nose, throat, chest, stomach, thighs, feet. When she finished her examination she announced: "You may get into bed. Do you have any questions?"

"Just one," said Pete. "Why did you knock?"

275.   A friend of mine was going around town, his mouth open, gasping for breath, his eyes popping out. So he went to the doctor, and the doctor told him he had only three months to live. He decided therefore to spend all his money. He bought everything he could think of. Then one day he ambled into a haberdashery shop and said, "Give me a dozen shirts, size 14½ in the neck, 32 in the sleeves."

"Wait a minute," said the salesperson, "you'd better let me measure your neck." He threw a tape measure around my friend's neck.

"You need a size 16," he announced. "If you took a 14½, you'd be going around all the time with your mouth open, gasping for breath, your eyes popping out."

276.   Thoroughly steeped in ethics, a physician always insisted on the presence of a third party in the room whenever he examined a female patient.

Near the close of a busy afternoon, he wearily motioned a couple into the examining room. The woman complained of pains in her lower abdomen, and submitted to examination reluctantly. The man looked on with unfeigned interest.

When he had finished, the doctor prescribed some medicine, and the woman jumped up from the table, dressed hurriedly, and ran out of the room.

"Your wife's certainly lively," commented the doctor. "She'll be all right in a few days."

"My *wife?*" said the man. "I never saw her before, Doc. I was wondering why you called me in here with you."

277.   It was 3 o'clock on a cold, rainy morning when the doctor was awakened by an emergency phone call. Struggling out of bed, he pulled on his clothes, went out to his car, and finally got it started.

The hospital was miles across town, and it took the haggard doctor nearly an hour to get there, sliding sideways over the ice most of the way. When at last he arrived and examined the girl who was ill, he discovered she had nothing more than a severe cold.

"Why didn't you call me in the daytime?" the doctor inquired.

"We're poor people, sir, and not able to pay much," the father explained, "so we thought we'd call when you weren't too busy."

Do-it-yourself

278.   One of these days somebody's going to come up with a book on "How to Get Out of Doing it Yourself." That person is destined to make a fortune.

Doubt—Doubts

279.   Following a knock on the door of an undergraduate's room at a university, a voice asked: "May I come in? This is the room I had when I was at college." He was invited in.

"Yes," he went on musingly. "Same old room. Same old furniture. Same old view from the window. Same old closet."

He opened the closet door. There stood a girl, looking scared.

"That is my sister," said the present occupant of the room.

"Yes," replied the visitor. "Same old story."

Dream—Dreams—Dreaming

280. Two fellows were discussing their dreams, and one said to the other: "Sam, did I ever dream last night—what a dream! I went to Disneyland, went on the Pirates of the Caribbean, ate everything from popcorn to peanuts, saw all the special shows—It was the greatest dream in the world!"

The other fellow said, "You're kidding. That's a dream? I had a much better one last night. I dreamed I went to a party, and I had Farah Fawcett on one arm and Kristie Brinkley on the other."

The first fellow said, "Gee, why didn't you call me?"

"I did," replied the other, "but your wife said you had gone to Disneyland."

281. In his wild imagination, he lived the lives of famous people, enjoyed their celebrity status, and socialized with their closest friends. His family became concerned with his more frequent "escapes from reality" and encouraged him to see a psychiatrist.

After several sessions, the psychiatrist announced, "Congratulations, Mr. Jones, you're a healed man."

"What a lousy cure," responded his patient. "Before I was famous and now I'm a nobody."

Drinking

282. *Little girl:* "Mama! Daddy and I stopped on my way home. I had a Coke and daddy had a glass of water with an olive in it."

283. After months at sea, the sailor hit port and headed for the nearest tavern. Pointing to a patron who lay prone on the floor, he instructed the barkeeper, "Give me a shot of that."

284. In an Ohioan city there is a tavern called "The Office." Should one stop in after work and find he'll be late getting home he can truthfully call up and tell his wife that he's been delayed at the office.

285. Two lumberjacks were drinking together at a bar

when suddenly one lurched backward off his stool and lay flat on the floor without moving a muscle.

"One thing about Tom," said the other to the bartender, "he knows when to stop."

286. A young bride of three months complained to her mother about her husband's continued drinking habits.

"If you knew he drank, why did you marry him?" she was asked.

"I didn't know he drank," the girl replied, "until one night he came home sober!"

287. It was at an important local dance that Mrs. Brown found it necessary to protest to Mr. Brown.

"Do you know," she said, "you've been to the bar six times this evening?"

"That's all right, my dear," he replied. "I tell everybody I'm getting something for you."

288. "Why do you beg?"

"The truth is I beg to get money for booze."

"Why do you drink?"

"To give me the courage to beg."

289. Toulouse-Lautrec, the French painter, was a heavy drinker who always had a bottle handy.

On one occasion, a friend berated him for his drunkenness.

"How can you drink so much?" he demanded.

"I do not drink so much," replied the artist. "I only drink very little—very often."

290. Two waiters were standing at a table over which a loaded customer had fallen asleep. Said one:

"I've already awakened him twice. Now I'm going to awaken him for the third time."

"Why don't you throw him out?" asked the other waiter.

"I can't do that," said the first waiter. "I got a good thing going for me. Every time I wake him up he pays his bill."

291. The preacher was having a heart-to-heart talk with a backslider of his flock, whose drinking invariably led to quarreling with his neighbors, and occasional shotgun blasts at some of them.

"Can't you see, Ben," intoned the parson, "that not one good thing comes out of this drinking?"

"Well, I sort of disagree there," replied the backslider. "It makes me miss the folks I shoot at."

292.   A shipping clerk went to his doctor and complained of a pain in his leg. After one glance at the leg the doctor asked the patient: "How long have you been walking around in this condition?"

Clerk: "Two weeks."

Doctor: "For heaven's sake young man, you have a broken leg! Why didn't you come to me sooner?"

Clerk: "Well, doc, I would have, but every time I say something is wrong with me my wife says I have to give up drinking."

293.   A well-dressed man came into the cocktail lounge each evening. He would be alone but always ordered two martinis. First he would drink one, then move over and drink the other.

The bartender's curiosity got the best of him, so one evening he asked the reason why two cocktails. The man explained that one was his and the other for his "best friend" who went west for his health. Then a few weeks later the man came in as usual but ordered only one martini. The bartender very solemnly asked, "What . . . only one? Did your friend pass away?"

The man replied, "Oh! No! I'm on the wagon."

Drug Store

294.   *Customer:* "Give me some of that prepared monoaceticacidester of salicylicacid."

Druggist: "Do you mean aspirin?"

Customer: "Yeah! I never can think of that name."

295.   A man with a worried look on his face ran into a drug store and asked the druggist if she knew a way to stop the hiccoughs. Without any warning the druggist slapped him in the face. Amazed and angry, the young man demanded that the druggist explain her unusual behavior.

"Well," said the druggist, "you don't have the hiccoughs now do you?"

"No," answered the young man, "but my wife out in the car still does."

296.   The drug store in a small town was closed down by its creditors. As he left the premises for the last time, the saddened proprietor paused long enough to tack this sign on the front door:

"Our doors are locked. The following services, formerly available here, may be had elsewhere from now on: *Ice-water* at fountain in the park. *General information* from the Chamber Office. *Change of a dollar* at the bank. *Matches and scratch pads* at the hotel. *Magazines for browsing* from the doctor. *Bus information* at the terminals. And *loafing* at any other location of your own choosing."

Drunkenness. See also Drinking

297.   "Well, you can't say I made any noise coming in last night."

"No, but the men who were carrying you did."

298.   "Why are you crying, little man?" said the old gent to a small boy.

"Father chewed me out for doing a crossword puzzle."

"Good gracious! Why?"

"Well, sir, one clue was a word of three letters meaning what is drunk every night—and I put *'dad'*!"

299.   A college professor was invited to the Dean's house for cocktails. Later, realizing that he had exceeded his normal capacity, the prof was determined that no one should be aware of his indiscretion. As the party neared its conclusion, the wife of the Dean decided to show the latest addition to her family, and presently a nurse appeared carrying a bassinet containing twins. The prof looked into the bassinet and, trying to sound as normal as possible, said, "My, what a beautiful baby."

E

Economics

300. The 1980 Presidential Campaign contained a heavy emphasis on economic issues. Ronald Reagan warned of the coming of another depression if America continued in its present path. President Carter reacted, "That shows how much he knows. This is a recession." That reaction gave Reagan, the communicator, a platform comment to build his campaign on. Reagan responded, "If Mr. Carter wants a definition, I'll give him one. Recession is when your neighbor loses his job, depression is when you lose yours, and recovery will be when Jimmy Carter loses his."

Education

301. "Say, Dad, did you go to Sunday school when you were a little boy?"

"Yes, son, regularly."

"Well, I'll bet it won't do me any good either."

302. "Yes, stamp collecting is educational," said the fond mother to the visitor. "For instance, where is Hungary, Eric?"

Without looking up from his stamp book, the young philatelist answered promptly: "Two pages in front of Italy."

303. *Father:* "I'm worried about your being at the bottom of the class."

Son: "Don't worry, Dad, they teach the same stuff at both ends."

304. A college professor was retiring after thirty years in the classroom. At a party, given in his honor, the educator was asked what he taught all those years.

"Even as we celebrate," the professor responded, "the college has a committee looking into that."

305. When asked the secret to motivating her students, the high school English teacher responded confidently: "I've never had a problem inspiring my students. Every class is notified at the beginning of the year that fifty percent of them will fail my class."

306. "The key to success," preached a motivational speaker, "is to read, read, read."

"What should we read?"

"Well," responded the speaker, "find out what unsuccessful people are reading . . . and don't read it."

307. The fifth grade teacher was reviewing the history lesson with his class. "Who can tell me who discovered America?"

Sally quickly raised her hand and said proudly, "Four fathers."

Embarrassment

308. A famous playwright volunteered his services to direct his son's school play. It was a simple two-act play but the real challenge was keeping the youngsters in line. Frustrated with the children's lack of cooperation, he blurted, "Everyone sit down! Now, would all the boys with small male parts please raise your hand."

309. When Anne Morrow Lindbergh was a child, her family invited John D. Rockefeller for tea. Concerned Anne might say something about Rockefeller's big nose, Mrs. Morrow reminded her several times, "Please don't say anything about his nose." Anne assured her mother she would keep silent.

When Rockefeller arrived, Anne greeted him politely and went off to play. Relieved, Mrs. Morrow poured her guest tea and asked, "Mr. Rockefeller, would you like some cream in your nose?"

Employer–Employee

310. Pity your boss. The poor guy has to get up early to see who comes in late.

311. If there were more self-starters, the boss wouldn't have to be a crank.

312. If at first you don't succeed, you're probably not related to the boss.

313. Is there anything so embarrassing as watching the boss doing something you told her couldn't be done?

314. When a secretary says the office staff is having a picnic, it may just mean that the boss is on vacation.

315. *Boss:* "This is just a suggestion. You don't have to follow it unless you want to keep your jobs."

316. "Have you an opening for a genius?"
"Yes, and don't slam the door on the way out."

317. "Miss Jones," said the baffled office manager, "how do you do it? You've been here two weeks, and you're already one month behind!"

318. *Interviewer:* "Young man, do you think you can handle a variety of work?"
Job hunter: "I ought to be able to. I've had 12 different jobs in less than six months."

319. The boss was pointing out to her secretary several errors she had made during the day, when she interrupted with, "Ms. Jones, it's two minutes past five and you're annoying me on my own time."

320. "Do you believe in life after death?" an employer asked an employee.
"Oh, yes, sir," was the reply.
"Ah, then everything is in order, because after you had gone to your grandfather's funeral yesterday, he came here to see you."

321. Then there was the dejected employee who came home one evening and slumped into a chair.

"Well," he said resignedly, "the worst has happened."

"Why, whatever happened, dear?" his wife asked anxiously.

"The boss called me in at quitting time and gave me the business."

322. A young woman, tired of working for others, went into business for herself. Later a friend asked her how it was to be her own boss.

"I don't know," she replied. "The police won't let me park in front of my own place of business; tax collectors tell me how to keep books; my banker tells me how much balance I must maintain; freight agents tell me how my goods must be packed; customers tell me how my goods must be made; federal, state, county and local agencies tell me how to keep records; the union tells me whom I can employ and how and when; and on top of that, I just got married."

323. During the noontime recreational activities the president of the corporation mounted the platform, accompanied by an overall-clad man off the assembly line, and made this speech.

"Ladies and gentlemen, you are about to see how American industry rewards those who are conscientious and hard-working. This man standing beside me has been with the company less than a year, during which time his unusual qualities have earned him salary increases in excess of one hundred dollars a week. I have watched him closely, observed with great pleasure the manner in which he has pitched in and gotten things done. Therefore, I am pleased to announce that starting this very afternoon he gets out of his work clothes, comes into the executive branch, and takes over an office with the title of Executive Vice President in Charge of Policy at an annual wage of eighty thousand dollars. Congratulations to you, sir."

The worker shook the extended hand and said: "Gee, thanks, Dad."

Employment

324. "For this job we want someone who is responsible."
"That's for me. Everywhere I've worked, whenever something went wrong, I was responsible."

325. *Shopper:* "Why, Mr. Smith, you are back again as sales clerk! I thought you were now an insurance salesperson."
Smith: "You made the same mistake I did."

326. "Do I detect the odor of liquor on your breath?" a stingy boss asked his sales manager.
"You do," admitted the sales manager. "I've just been celebrating the twentieth anniversary of the last raise you gave me."

327. On the job application blank was the question, "Have you ever been arrested?" The applicant put down, "No."
The next question was "Why"—meant for those who had been arrested. Not realizing this, the applicant put down, "Never been caught."

328. A secretary was applying for a new job. Under "office experience" on the application blank she wrote: "I'm familiar with all the important phases of office procedure–including bowling, crossword puzzles, coffee breaks, personal letter-writing and collection-taking."

329. "What does your husband do?" one wife asked another.
"He's an expediter."
"What's that?"
"Well, it's hard to explain but if we women did what he does, they'd call it nagging."

330. The president called in eight of his department heads for confidential discussion. "I understand," he said, "that all of you have been dating Miss Jones, the receptionist. I want the truth now. How many of you have been taking her out?"
Seven of the executives raised their hands and looked sheep-

ish. The big boss glared at the eighth man and intoned: "Are you *sure* that you are telling the truth?"

"Yes, I am," was the reply.

"All right then," came the punchline. "*You* fire her."

331. The Smithsons went away for their summer vacation and gave their maid, Jane, a month's wages before leaving. On their return four weeks later, Jane demanded higher wages, or she would leave.

Mrs. Smithson was horrified. "Gracious," she exclaimed, "you've only just had a month off with full pay. You should consider yourself very fortunate."

"That's just it," she replied. "You paid me all that money for doing nothing, so how can you expect me to do all this work now for the same wages?"

332. The story is told of the owner of a large department store who went over his books and discovered that his most trusted employee had stolen over a million dollars from the firm.

"I want no scandal," the owner said. "I'll just fire you and forget about the entire matter."

The employee replied, "So you're going to fire me. True, I robbed your concern of quite a tidy sum. I now have yachts, a country mansion, a town house, jewelry, and every luxury you can think of. I don't need a thing, so why hire somebody else and have them start from scratch?"

333. A man applying for a job asked the interviewer whether the company would pay for his hospital insurance. The interviewer said the worker would have to pay for it but it was deducted from his check.

"The last place I worked the company paid for it," he said.

"Did they pay for your life insurance too?" the interviewer asked.

"Sure they did," the man said. "Not only that, but we got unlimited sick leave, severance pay, three weeks' vacation, a Christmas bonus, coffee breaks . . ."

"Then why did you leave such a perfect place?" the interviewer asked.

"The company folded," the man replied.

334.   A man knocked at the heavenly gate,
His face was scarred and old.
He stood before the Man of Fate
For admission to the fold.
"What have you done," St. Peter asked,
"To gain admission here?"
"I've been an executive, Sir," he said,
"For many and many a year."
The pearly gates swung open wide;
St. Peter touched the bell.
"Come in and choose your harp," he said,
"You've had your share of hell."

Author Unknown

335.   "To get ahead in this organization," the department manager told her employees, "you've got to do more than show up for work. We need to see some enthusiasm for what you do. Start getting excited about getting up in the morning. Enjoy enthusiastic times with your family, and, for goodness sake, do everything on your job with enthusiasm."

Three days later, one of her employees showed up two hours late for work. Looking at her watch the supervisor asked, "Is this what you consider coming to work enthusiastically?"

"Let me explain," the embarrassed employee responded. "I jumped out of bed with enthusiasm, sang enthusiastically in the shower, enthusiastically ate my breakfast, and then gave my wife an enthusiastic good-by kiss—and well, that's why I'm late."

Epitaph—Epitaphs

336.   Occasionally, professional people have taken as their epitaphs phrases from their earthly work.

One doctor, for example, finally flouted the rule that prohibits physicians from advertising. She had the following carved on her headstone: *"Office Upstairs."*

Not to be outdone, a lawyer's gravestone read: *"Final Decree."*

Evolution

337. A man, in his anxiety to refute evidence that he is a monkey, manages to further the belief that he is an ass.

338. Somebody must take a chance. The monkeys who did became humans, and the monkeys who didn't are still jumping around in trees making faces at the monkeys who did.

Excuse—Excuses

339. The story is told of the farmer who called at the home of his neighbor and asked if he might borrow a rope. "Oh, good and faithful neighbor, I must regretfully refuse of you this simple favor," spoke the man. "The rope you request cannot be given, for I use it to tie up my milk."

"But surely," replied the would-be borrower, "milk cannot be tied up with a rope?"

"You're right," the refuser said. "But when one does not want to do a thing, one reason is as good as another."

340. A woman joined a local health club but after the first day requested her membership be refunded.

"Is there a problem?" asked the proprietor.

"Yes," she replied. "Your floors are so low I can't touch my toes."

Expert—Experts

341. The fellow had spent his entire life studying goldfish. At a meeting of the Goldfish Lovers of America he was asked how one could tell the difference between a male goldfish and female goldfish.

"That's simple," said the man of knowledge. "Male goldfish will eat only male worms."

"But how," persisted the questioner, "can you tell the difference between male worms and female worms?"

"Haven't the slightest idea," he replied. "I'm not an expert on worms . . . just goldfish."

342. A kind-hearted motorist saw a man struggling to change a tire alongside the highway. There was a dirty smear across his red face where he had wiped off the sweat with dirty hands. His tie was undone, his shirt collar askew, and obviously he had also wiped his hands on his once-white shirt. Close to him stood a slight woman, immaculately neat, and arguing angrily.

"Look, friend," said the kind-hearted motorist. "I've changed a lot of tires. Is there anything I can do to help?"

"There sure is," replied the man with the tire tool. "My wife is an expert, too. If you will just do all the arguing with her about how this tire ought to be changed, I can concentrate on the dirty work and get the job done."

F

Failure

343.   The tramps sat with their backs against an oak tree. Before them was a rippling stream. Although the day was delightful, one of them was disconsolate.

"You know, Jim," he mused, "this business of tramping your way through life is not what it's cracked up to be. Think it over—nights on park benches or in a cold barn. Traveling on freight trains and always dodging the police. Being kicked from one town to another. Wondering where your next meal is coming from. Wandering, unwanted everywhere, sneered at by your fellow men." His voice trailed off as he sighed heavily. His companion shifted his position slightly.

"Well," observed the second tramp, "if that's the way you feel about it, why don't you go and find yourself a job?"

The first tramp sat up with a jerk, opening his mouth in amazement. "What?" he exclaimed. "And admit I'm a failure?"

Fair play

344.   One day, many years ago, two young fellows were in a quarrel, and it had signs of becoming serious. Abraham Lincoln, himself a young man but with an earnest desire for fair play, was called upon to decide the difficulty. One of the combatants, who had been defeated in the decision, and above whom the towering Lincoln stood head and shoulders, boastfully threatened Lincoln.

"See here, Lanky, I'll lick you!" he shouted.

Abe looked down comically at the small challenger. "All right," he said, "but let's fight fair. You are so small there isn't much of you for me to hit, but I am so big, you can't help hitting me. So you make a chalkmark on me that will show just your size. When we fight, you must be sure to hit me inside this mark or it won't be fair."

The idea was so ridiculous, the little bully began to laugh, and the quarrel ended as a joke.

Faith

345.   Two nuns went to work as nurses in a local nursing home. They ran out of gas driving to work one morning and sat stranded alongside a busy highway. The decision was made to walk to a nearby gas station but they had no container in which to put the gasoline. One of the women remembered a bedpan she had placed in the trunk of the car. Upon retrieving the unusual container, the gas was put into the bedpan and carried carefully back to the car. Just as the nuns began carefully pouring the gasoline from the bedpan into the gas tank, a family drove by and stared in disbelief. Finally, the father blurted, "That's what I call acting in faith."

346.   "My message this morning," began the recent seminary graduate, "is on the relationship between fact and faith. It is a fact that this is Sunday morning. It is also a fact that you are here and that I am ready to speak to you. It is faith that makes me believe you will remember what I have to say."

Fame

347.   "What's your name?" asked the store manager of the young boy who was applying for a job.

"Ford," replied the lad.

"And your first name?"

"Henry."

"Henry Ford, eh?" queried the manager with a smile. "That's a pretty well-known name."

The boy looked pleased. "Yes, sir, it should be," he replied proudly. "I've been delivering groceries around town for two years now."

348. A small boy went with his family for a visit of several days in New York City and of all the sights they saw his big favorite was the majestic statue of General Sherman on horseback at Fifth Avenue and 59th Street.

He asked to be taken back to the statue several times and, every time he went, he asked countless questions about the great Northern general. On the trip back to his home he was still cross-examining his father on the details of Sherman's deeds in the Civil War.

"But, Daddy, there's one thing I don't understand," he said finally. "Who is that man who was sitting on General Sherman?"

Familiarity

349. An editor, weary of the abuse following his editorials, ran the Ten Commandments in his editorial column.

A few days later came a letter: "Cancel my subscription. You're getting too personal."

350. The doctor had been called to look over Grandma, who had been complaining of aches and pains. He gave her a thorough going-over.

After he left, Grandma seemed to perk up a bit. "What did you say was the name of that new minister?" she asked.

"That wasn't the minister—that was the doctor," she was told.

"Hmmm, I thought he was a bit familiar for a minister," Grandma replied.

Family

351. A guy we know was the youngest of 14 children. He was 20 years old before he found there were other parts of a chicken besides the gravy.

352. *Pompous speaker:* "There are 100 jails in this state and I'm proud to say that no members of my family have ever been in one of them."

Voice from the rear: "And which one is that?"

353. *Customer:* "I want an alarm clock that will wake father without arousing the whole family."

Clerk: "We have only the ordinary kind that will awaken the entire family without disturbing father."

354. "So you're not bothered any more with relatives coming and staying?" asked Jim.

"No," answered Tom with satisfaction. "I borrow money from the rich ones and lend it to the poor ones, and none of them come back."

355. The warden of one of the more advanced prisons began to feel sorry for one of the prisoners. On visitors' day, while most of the prisoners' visited with family and friends and such, this fellow sat alone in his cell.

One visiting day, the warden called him into the office. "Ben," he said kindly, "I notice you never have any callers. Don't you have any friends—or family?"

"Oh sure," replied Ben happily, "but they're all in here."

Farm—Farmer—Farming

356. A farmer shipped two rabbits east by motor transportation. The crate arrived with two rabbits. That's fast transportation!

357. A man stopped by a booming oil field in southern Kentucky to give a lift to a man on his way to the county seat. They drove through once beautiful farm land now scarred by bulldozers and drilling rigs, cluttered with pumps and storage tanks. Guessing that his passenger was a farmer living in the area, the driver steered the conversation to the tall tales he had heard of quick riches for both speculators and farmers.

The local man acknowledged that many of the stories were founded on fact. "You own a farm here?" the driver asked. "Yeah" was the reply.

"Any oil wells on it?" "Yeah, three good'uns and they say they'll make 300 barrels a day."

"What in the world are you going to do with all the money

you'll be getting?" The farmer gazed for a moment across a machine-scarred field and answered, "Why I'm gonna buy me a farm that ain't got no oil on it."

358. A midwest farmer was describing his lifestyle to a touring group of city folks. "One of the benefits of this profession," he explained, "is that we have built-in weather predictions."

"What do you mean by that?" asked one inquisitive visitor.

"When the cows are standing," the farmer explained, "it means no rain is likely for the next twenty-four hours. When they're lying down, it means it's going to rain."

"On our bus trip," another visitor piped in, "I saw half the herd standing and the other half lying down. What does this mean?"

The farmer flashed a smile and answered, "That means half of 'em are wrong."

359. Murphy's laws have undergone revision in the Midwest. The farming community now has their own including:

* The bean market will go up 20 cents the day after you sell.
* If you've got a 12-row planter, you'll finish the field with 13 rows to plant.
* It only rains on the day you load livestock.
* The farm implement dealer lacks just one part. Yours.
* "Reworked" means "repainted."
* A dropped bolt will roll under the truck to its exact geographic center.

360. A novice young farmer was looking for some advice and asked an experienced farmer, "What would be good to plant in an area that gets very little rain, has too much late afternoon sun, has clay soil, and lies on a rocky ledge?" Replied the farmer, "How about a flag pole?"

Father—Son

361. *Thoughtful mother:* "If my son is getting as much out of college as his college is getting out of me, he will be a success."

362. "My son's letters always send me to the dictionary," bragged the father of a Harvard undergraduate.

"You're lucky," replied his friend. "My son's letters always send me to the bank."

363. A father was berating his son who was reluctant to do his homework. "When Abraham Lincoln was your age," the father lectured, "he walked 10 miles to school every day and then studied by the light of the fire in his log cabin."

"So what?" the boy rejoined. "When John Kennedy was your age, he was President!"

364. Joe Garagiola, in his book *It's Anybody's Ballgame*, shares an insightful story involving baseball great, Yogi Berra.

Yogi was already a star when he sat talking with teammate Charlie Keller in the Yankee clubhouse. "Do you remember the first time we met?" Yogi asked Keller.

"I sure do," Keller replied. "I remember seeing you walk through that door in your Navy uniform."

Yogi nodded and said, "I'll bet you didn't think I was a ballplayer."

At that point, clubhouse manager Pete Sheehy chimed in, "I didn't even think you were a sailor."

Joe Garagiola, It's Anybody's Ballgame
(Contemporary Books)

Fishing

365. It's a crime to catch a fish in some lakes and a miracle in lots of others.

366. A thoughtful wife is one who has the pork chops ready when her husband comes home from a fishing trip.

367. A man who will sit on a pier all day waiting to catch a fish will complain if his wife has dinner 10 minutes late.

368. A fisherman was lugging a fish twice his size when he met another fisherman with a half dozen small ones on a string.

"Howdy," said the first fisherman, dropping the huge fish and waiting for a comment.

The fellow fisherman stared and stared. Then he said calmly, "Just caught the one, eh?"

369.   "Young man," said the stern moralist to the boy fishing on the creek bank, "your time must not be very valuable. I've been watching you two hours and you haven't had a single bite."

"Well, stranger," the lad replied, "I consider my time too valuable to waste two hours of it watching another guy fishing when he isn't catching anything!"

370.   An old-timer sat on the river bank, obviously awaiting a nibble, though the fishing season had not officially opened. The game warden stood behind him quietly for several minutes. "You the game warden?" the old-timer inquired.

"Yup."

Unruffled, the old man began to move the fishing pole from side to side. Finally, he lifted the line out of the water. Pointing to a minnow wriggling on the end of the line, he said, "Just teaching him how to swim."

371.   Two ardent fishermen met on their vacation and began swapping stories about the different places they had fished, the kind of tackle used, the best bait, and finally about some of the fish they had caught.

One of them told of a vicious battle he once had with a 300-pound salmon. The other man listened attentively. He frankly admitted he had never caught anything quite that big. However, he told about the time his hook snagged a lantern from the depths of a lake. The lantern carried a tag proving it was lost back in 1912. But the strangest thing of all was the fact that it was a waterproof lantern and the light was still lit.

For a long time the first man said nothing. Then he took one long last draw on his cigarette before rubbing it out in the ash tray.

"I'll tell you what I'll do," he said slowly. "I'll take 200 pounds off my fish, if you'll put out the light in your lantern."

Folly

372.   There's no fool like an old fool—you can't beat experience.

Food

373. *Groom:* "The two best things I cook are meat loaf and apple dumplings."

Bride: "Which is this?"

374. A fellow walked into a restaurant, ordered three hamburgers, two steaks, a shrimp salad, fried rice, a side order of dill pickles and ice cream.

The waitress was amazed. "Boy!" she exclaimed. "You sure like food."

"Matter of fact," said the customer, "I hate it. I'm just crazy about bicarbonate of soda."

Forgetfulness

375. *Husband (who's forgotten) to wife:* "How do you expect me to remember your birthday when you never look any older?"

376. *Professor:* "Jones, can you tell me who built the Sphinx?"

Student: "I did know, Ms. Smith, but I've forgotten."

Professor: "Great guns, what a calamity! The only person living who knows, and he has forgotten!"

Forgiveness

377. In his autobiography Mark Twain concluded a tirade against a publisher, who had once swindled him outrageously, on a note of forgiveness.

"He has been dead a quarter of a century now," Twain wrote. "I feel only compassion for him, and if I could send him a fan I would."

Frustration

378. A most frustrated person was the cannibal who bought a new boomerang and had a terrible time throwing the old one away.

G

Gambling. See also Bet—Bets—Betting

379. What often keeps a man from making a fast buck is a slow horse.

380. Lady Godiva was the world's greatest gambler because she put everything on a horse.

381. *Sign over a tailor shop in Las Vegas:*
WHILE YOU'RE HERE, WHY DON'T YOU
HAVE YOUR CLOTHES CLEANED TOO.

382. Have you heard the one about the lawyer who drove her $5,000 Cadillac to Las Vegas and came back on a $100,000 Greyhound?

383. At a Las Vegas gambler's funeral, the speaker asserted, "Spike is not dead, he only sleeps."
From among the gambling friends who were attending came a voice, "I got $100 that says he's dead."

384. A beautiful chapel under construction stopped an admiring passer-by. He fell into conversation with the building supervisor, and many adjectives later, asked: "What denomination is it?"
"Don't know," said the supervisor, "we're building it on speculation."

385. Two men were commenting on a friend's bad luck at the horse races.
"Funny," said one, "how lucky Harry is at cards and how unlucky at the track."

"Nothing funny about it," replied the other. "They won't let him shuffle the horses."

386.   "Mary," said a gambler to her friend, "I must tell you about this guy I met yesterday. He's figured out a system whereby a whole family can live without money."

The other gambler looked up eagerly. "Does it work?"

"No," admitted her friend sadly, "but that's the only loophole in her system."

387.   A young married couple spending a week at a famous spa had nothing but bad luck, and on the sixth day were down to their last two dollars and a ticket to the local race track.

"Let me go out there alone today," said the young man. "I've got a hunch."

He picked a 40-to-one shot in the first race, and won. Every succeeding race was won by a long shot on which he had a bet. At the end of the afternoon, he had amassed more than 10 thousand dollars.

On his way back to the hotel, he stopped off at one of the gambling casinos to cash in further on his good luck. Within an hour he had run his bankroll up to a neat 40 thousand dollars at roulette. On the point of leaving, he had a new hunch and the entire 40 thousand went on black.

The ball bounced, rolled and settled. The croupier called "Red!"

The young man made his way back to his hotel room, sat down, and lit a cigarette. His wife asked, "How did you make out?"

"I lost two dollars," he nonchalantly replied.

Garden—Gardens—Gardening

388.   The best way to enjoy a beautiful, productive garden is to live next door to one, and cultivate your neighbor.

389.   The easiest way to tell the difference between young plants and weeds is to pull up everything. If they come up again, they're weeds.

390.   "My garden was such a success this year," boasted a country gardener, "that my neighbor's chickens took first prize at the poultry show."

391.   An ad in a London newspaper read: "Sprinkle this magic mixture on your flowerbeds and nothing will grow, thus leaving you with plenty of leisure for other things."

392.   A man who was new in the suburbs strolled over to observe a neighbor who was digging a hole in his backyard and said, "That's a pretty deep hole. What are you going to put in it?"

"I am replanting some of my garden seeds," was the quick response.

"But you surely don't need such a deep hole to plant a few seeds," the new neighbor said incredulously.

"I surely do," replied the digger. "The seeds are all inside one of your chickens."

393.   A wife who was always nagging her husband to mow the lawn hit on a sneaky new way to annoy him. He got home one afternoon and found her out cutting the grass herself with the new power motor. She was, in short, shaming him before the whole neighborhood.

Furious, he took over and finished the job. When he put the mower away, he disconnected the spark plug so as to make sure she wouldn't be able to pull such a stunt a second time.

Several weeks went by and again he came home only to find her out mowing the lawn again.

"There was something wrong with the mower," she told him, "but I called a repair man and he fixed it. And he only charged $25."

Gift—Gifts

394.   "How'd your wife like those back scratchers I sent her for Christmas?"

"You mean that's what they were? She's been making me eat salad with them."

395.   A woman who lived far beyond her three-score-and-ten years had been in the habit of having a birthday party every year. Her friends and relatives always remembered her with little gifts which were usually in the form of knick-knacks for the house.

Finally arriving at the age of ninety, the old lady was asked by a friend what she wanted for her birthday this year.

"Give me a kiss," was the reply, "so I won't have to dust it."

Giving

396. When it comes to giving, some people stop at nothing.

397. 'Tis much better to give than to receive—and it's deductible.

398. The trouble with some folks who give until it hurts is that they are so sensitive to pain.

399. A recent appeal by a famous neurological institute asked doctors to bequeath their brains for research.

It ended: "any contributions, however small, will be gratefully appreciated."

Golf

400. By the time a man can afford to lose a golf ball, he can't hit that far.

401. Golf is a lot like taxes—you drive hard to get to the green and then wind up in the hole.

402. One of the quickest ways to meet new people is to pick up the wrong ball on a golf course.

403. Funny, isn't it? Men blame fate for other accidents, but feel personally responsible when they make a hole in one.

404. "I see where a Russian says he has invented a game which closely resembles golf."

"That must be the game my husband has been playing for years."

405.   "I'd move heaven and earth to be able to break 100 on this course," sighed Mac, the golfer.

"Try heaven," advised the caddie. "You've already moved most of the earth."

406.   An executive's wife kidded him about his devotion to the links. "If you keep spending so much time playing golf," she jested, "you won't have anything set aside for a rainy day."

"Never fear," he replied. "My desk is loaded with work I've got put aside for a rainy day."

407.   A woman was bemoaning the fact that her husband had left her for the sixth time.

"Never mind," consoled the neighbor. "He'll be back again."

"Not this time," sobbed the wife. "He's taken his golf clubs this time."

408.   A golfer, trying to get out of a trap, said to her competitor:

"The traps on this course are very annoying, aren't they?"

The second golfer, trying to putt, replied:

"They are, indeed, so would you please close yours?"

409.   He had just come in from a long afternoon at golf. His wife kissed him and remarked that their son had just come in, too.

"He says he's been caddying for you," she remarked.

"By golly," exclaimed the golfer, "no wonder that kid looked so familiar!"

410.   "Why don't you play golf with George any more?" Pete's wife asked him.

"Would you play with a fellow who puts down the wrong score and moves the ball when you aren't watching?" replied Pete.

"No," she replied, "I certainly wouldn't."

"Neither will George."

411.   Sam, innocent of all golfing lore, watched with interest the efforts of the man in the bunker to get himself out.

At last the ball rose in a cloud of sand, hovered in the air and then dropped on the green and rolled into the hole.

"Gosh," said Sam with a chuckle, "he'll have a tough time getting out of that one."

412. The minister was out on the course and thought that it might not be a bad time to slip in a quick moral observation to his partner.

"I have observed," he said, "that the best golfers are not addicted to bad language."

His partner swept a load of topsoil into space and, looking down, said: "What the hell have *they* got to swear about?"

413. Two golfing enthusiasts were discussing their scores in the locker room. "I can't understand it," said one disgustedly, "I've been playing golf for twenty years and I get worse every year. Believe it or not, last year I played worse than the year before. And the year before, I was worse than the last year."

"That's too bad," commented the other. "How are you doing now?"

"I am already," said the woman unhappily, "playing next year's game."

414. It was Saturday morning and while they were having breakfast, Mr. Smith suddenly announced that he didn't have to go to the office that morning.

"Well, don't think," said the wife, "that you're going to run off to play golf today and leave me alone with all this work to do."

"Why, golf is the furthest thing from my mind," replied the husband, gnawing at his breakfast, "and please pass me the putter."

415. All summer Paul watched Eddie give demonstrations on how to putt. Ed, who sometimes wears glasses, seldom missed a putt, even from the edge of the green. Finally, at the end of the summer, Paul asked how he holed out so accurately.

"Well," said Ed, "these glasses of mine are bifocals. When I line up a putt, I look through the edges of the two lenses so I see two balls, one small and one big, and two holes, one small and one big. Then it's simple. I just knock the small ball in the big hole."

416. The club's worst golfer was addressing his golf ball. He waggled his driver several times, missed three swings, and finally drove his ball about 20 feet. Looking up in exasperation he saw a squirrel hunter with a gun across his shoulder, who had stopped to watch him. "Look here!" shouted the member angrily. "Only golfers are allowed on this course!"

The stranger nodded, "I know it, mister," he replied. "But I won't say anything if you won't, either!"

417.   A group of golfers were putting on the green. Suddenly a ball dropped in their midst. One of the golfers winked at the others, and with her foot shoved the ball into the hole.

A few seconds later a very fat fellow came up to the hole, puffing and out of breath.

"Didja see the ball?" he asked anxiously.

The foursome responded: "Yes."

"Where is it?"

"It went in the hole."

The fat man looked at them unbelieving, walked up to the hole, reached down, picked up the ball. He gazed at it in astonishment, then ran down the fairway and at the top of his lungs shouted, "Hey, Joe. I got a nine."

418.   Norman Cousins tells about a priest who was playing golf and he had difficulty in hitting the ball over a small pond. After he put five balls in the water, he hesitated before teeing up again, then said to his caddy: "I know what I'm doing wrong. I just forgot to pray before each shot, that was all." He prayed, then swung at the ball—and it traveled about twenty yards in a loop right into the water. "Father," asked the caddy, "might I make a suggestion?" "Certainly, son" the priest said. "Well, father," the caddy said, "the next time you pray, keep your head down."

419.   Golfing great Jack Nicklaus once asked baseball pro Henry Aaron, "What kind of golfer are you?"

"It took me seventeen years to get three thousand hits in baseball," Aaron answered. "I did it in one afternoon on the golf course."

420.   Bob Toski, a golf teaching professional, tells the story of a golfer who had come to the 17th hole with only two golf balls left, an old one and a new one. The tee shot had to pass over a fairly large body of water and the man scratched his head, wondering which of the balls to use.

As he stood on the tee mulling this problem, the golfer heard a voice boom out of the heavens: "Have confidence, play . . . the . . . new . . . ball!"

He looked around and saw no one. So he teed up the new ball and addressed it. As he waggled the club, he again heard the voice from the heavens: "Take . . . a . . . practice . . . swing."

Practice swing? What was he to do, other than follow this celestial advice. He stepped away from the ball and took the practice swing. He was brimming with confidence as he read-dressed the ball.

But just before he began his swing, the voice boomed again: "Play . . . the . . . old . . . ball."

421. Bob Hope is convinced Gerry Ford was the first person to make golf a contact sport. When he yelled 'fore!' says Hope, "you never knew if he was telling people to get out of the way or predicting how many spectators he was going to hit."

Government

422. *First farmer:* "Don't think much of that weather prophet the government's got on the radio."

Second farmer: "Well, let's don't do any complainin' about it. Just think how bad it would be if the government started regulatin' the weather instead of predictin' it!"

423. At the check-out counter in a New England supermarket an elderly man unfolded, endorsed and handed to the clerk a rumpled government check on which was plainly printed: "Do not fold, spindle or mutilate."

The clerk looked at it, frowned and said, "You shouldn't do that, Henry. The government doesn't like it."

The old man looked her straight in the eye and replied with emphasis, "Hazel, the government does some things I don't like, too."

Grandparent—Grandparents

424. A grandmother recently met her friend and started to ask, "Did I tell you about the cute thing my granddaughter said . . ."

But she was cut short with, "Before you start I warn you that I demand equal time—and I have sixteen grandchildren!"

425. There was a grandmother who was so tickled to learn that her grandchildren were coming for a week that she put a $5.00 bill in the collection plate at church. When they went home at the end of the week, her joy must have been double because that Sunday she put a $10.00 bill in the plate.

426. A wealthy old farmer was having a family reunion with his large family and as they all sat down to the table for a Sunday dinner, the old man looked around at his six big strapping sons and said:

"I don't see any grandchildren around this table of mine. I want you all to know that I will give $10,000 to the first one of you who presents me with a grandchild. We will now say grace."

When he raised his eyes again, he and his wife were the only ones at the table.

Gratitude

427. If you pick up a starving dog and make him prosperous, he will not bite you. This is the principal difference between a person and a dog.

428. An attractive young lady sat in her stalled auto, awaiting help. Two young men walked up and volunteered their aid.

"I'm out of gas," she lamented. "Could you push me to a gas station?"

They readily put their muscles to the rear of the car and rolled it several blocks. After a while, one looked up, exhausted, to see that they had just passed a filling station. "How come you didn't turn in?" he called.

"I never go there," the girl shouted back. "They don't give trading stamps."

H

Habit—Habits

429. "My wife has the worst habit of staying up until one or two o'clock in the morning, and I can't break her of it."

"What is she doing all that time?"

"Waiting for me to come home."

430. A reckless driver made a right turn from a left lane and collided with another car. The other driver angrily asked, "Why didn't you signal?"

Without a moment's hesitation, the driver replied, "I always turn here."

Happiness

431. Determining whether someone is happy or not can be difficult. Erma Bombeck has pinpointed why. She says, "We sing 'make a joyful noise unto the Lord' while our faces reflect the sadness of one who just buried a rich aunt who left everything to her pregnant hamster."

Heaven

432. Max Isaackson, in his book *Public Speaking and Other Coronary Threats,* shares a favorite story told to him by a minister friend. It seems there were four married couples on their way to Heaven. All had developed bad habits and it was very obvious to St. Peter, who met them at the Pearly Gates.

St. Peter looked at the first man and said, "You can't come in here now because you're a boozer and all YOU think about is drink, drink, drink. And I notice that even your wife's name is 'Ginny.' "

St. Peter then looked at the second man and exclaimed, "You can't come in here now, either, because you are a miser and all YOU think about is money, money, money, and I notice that YOUR wife's name is 'Penny.' "

The third man braced himself and he, too got a negative reaction. "You can't come in because you worship things that glitter and all you can think about is jewelry, jewelry, jewelry, and I see that YOUR wife's name is 'Ruby.' "

Hearing all of this, the fourth man turned to his wife and yelled, "COME ON, FANNIE, HE WON'T LET US IN, EITHER."

Honesty

433. A minister announced to the congregation that the topic for next week's sermon would be integrity. In preparation for the message, the congregation was asked to read the wisdom of Solomon found in Proverbs 32.

The next Sunday the minister began by asking the congregation how many had read the assigned scripture. Several hands flashed into the air.

"Just as I thought," said the minister, "there is no 32nd chapter in the book of Proverbs. Thereby, the need for this sermon on honesty."

Honeymoon

434. In the days before modern appliances an old lady in southern Georgia was busy kneading a huge batch of bread. Noticing that her wood fire needed replenishing, she hastily removed her hands from the dough and rushed to the wood pile where she chopped an armload of wood. As she returned her teenage daughter was standing nearby.

"Momma," she said dreamily. "How long does a honeymoon last?"

" 'Til there's dough on the axe handle, Honey," the old lady replied grimly, " 'Til there's dough on the axe handle."

Horse racing

435.   One man has discovered how to bring home money from the tracks. Instead of picking horses, he picks pockets.

436.   "I just crossed a horse with a fish."
"How did you do that?"
"I put a fin on a horse's nose."

437.   "Now, don't tell stories, Jimmy. You know your father never took you to the zoo in his whole life."
"Yes, he did, Mommy, and one of the animals paid twenty seven dollars!"

438.   *Spectator:* "My, but the horses in the next race have peculiar names."
Betting man: "Just wait until you hear what the losers call them after the race."

439.   Father looked up from his racing form and noticed the baby in the buggy. Turning to his wife he said, "Baby's nose is running again."
His wife snorted and snapped, "Don't you ever think of anything except horse races?"

440.   People certainly are a unique breed. They have always known that one horse can run faster than another, and yet they squander millions of dollars each year to see that simple fact demonstrated over and over again.

441.   "Father," asked the small boy, "which can go faster, horses or buses?"
"Buses, of course," replied the father impatiently.
"Then why," asked the boy, "don't you bet on the buses?"

442.   A westerner entered an eight-year-old horse in a race at an eastern track. Since the horse had never raced before, he went off at odds of 80 to 1. But he galloped home first by several lengths.
The stewards naturally were suspicious and called in the

owner. "How come you never raced this horse before?" they demanded. "After all, you've had him for eight years."

"Well, to tell you the truth," the westerner said sheepishly, "we couldn't catch him until he was seven."

Hospitality

443. The eager-to-please host turned to the guest of honor and gushed: "I suppose I can't offer you wine. You are the head of the Temperance League, aren't you?"

"No," he replied, "I'm head of the Anti-Vice League."

"Well," the flustered host explained, "I knew there was something I wasn't supposed to offer you."

444. A two-fisted ward boss named Pat Murphy sometimes received invitations to the parties and sometimes was left out. When one of the victory parties to which he had not been invited came off, Pat was almost the first man to appear.

"Why, Pat," said one of his friends, "How come you're here? I understand you were not invited."

"I know it," smiled the Irishman as he reached for a mug of beer and a sandwich, "but I thought I'd show up just the same, to prove I wasn't mad at not being asked."

Hospitals

445. Dr. Norman Cousins believes the responsibility for seeing humor lies with the patient. He wrote about his own experience while being hospitalized:

"When I was having breakfast, a nurse came in with a specimen bottle, and—when she wasn't looking—I took my apple juice, poured it into the bottle, and handed it to her.

"She looked at the bottle and said to me, 'My, we're a little cloudy today, aren't we?'—whereupon I took a big swig from the bottle and replied, "By George, you're right! Let's run it through again!"

Host—Guest

446. Don't try to make your guests feel at home. If they wanted to feel at home, they would have stayed there.

447. "Does your wife know you're bringing me home for dinner?"

448. *Visitor:* "Do you like reciting, dear?"
Child: "Oh, no, I hate it, really. But Mommy makes me do it when she wants people to go."

449. A famous politician had been visiting in the home of friends and the hour came for him to leave. After saying goodbye to the adults, he paused at the entrance where a little girl opened the door to let him out.

The honored guest bowed to her and said, "I am sorry, my little dear, to give you so much trouble."

She replied, "I wish, sir, it was to let you in."

450. One blistering hot day when they had guests for dinner, a mother asked her four-year-old son to say grace before the meal.

"But I don't know what to say," the boy exclaimed.

"Oh, just say what you hear me say," the mother replied.

Obediently, the boy bowed his head and murmured: "Oh, Lord, why did I invite those people here on a hot day like this?"

Hotel—Hotels

451. *Guest to bellhop:* "Quick! Run up to room 415 and see if I left my pajamas and razor in the bathroom. I'm waiting for a taxi to the airport."

Bellhop (five minutes later and out of breath): "Yes, sir, they're up there!"

452. A tall gaunt-looking man recently entered a small hotel in a town where several fires had occurred, and applied for a room at a price which entitled him to lodging on the top floor. Among his belongings the proprietor spotted a coil of rope, and asked what it was for.

"That's a fire escape," the man said. "I carry one with me so I can let myself down from the window without troubling anyone."

"That's a good plan," said the hotelowner, "but guests with personal fire escapes like that pay in advance at this hotel."

Hunting

453. Did you hear about the hunter who climbed through the fence with his gun cocked? He is survived by his wife, three children and a rabbit.

454. *Neophyte hunter:* "I shot an elk."
Friend: "How do you know it was an elk?"
Hunter: "By his membership card."

455. An exhausted hunter stumbled into the arms of a fellow hunter: "Am I glad to see you. I've been lost for two days."
"Don't get too excited, friend. I've been lost for two weeks."

456. "Yes," asserted the big game hunter at a cocktail party, "I used to shoot tigers in Africa."
One of his listeners protested, "But there are no tigers on that continent."
"Of course not," glibly replied the hunter, "I shot them all."

457. An avid duck hunter decided to exercise his shooting skill with big game. As he prepared for his first elephant hunt, the hunter was forced to quit. He got a hernia from carrying the decoys.

Husband—Wife

458. When a man or woman displays strength of character in their own home, it's called stubbornness.

459. "How can you talk to me like that," he wailed, "after I've given you the best years of my life?"
"Yeah?" returned the wife. "And who made them the best years of your life?"

460. "Your husband says he leads a dog's life."
"Yes, it's very similar. He comes in with muddy feet, makes himself comfortable by the fire, and waits to be fed."

461. *Maid:* "Your husband, ma'am, is lying unconscious in the hall with a piece of paper in his hand and a large box by his side!"

Mrs. Green (*joyfully*): "Oh, then my new outfit has arrived!"

462. After a very trying day at the office, the husband was enjoying his pipe and reading the evening paper. His wife, who was working on a crossword puzzle, suddenly called out, "John, what is a female sheep?"

"Ewe," replied her husband . . . And that's how the fight began.

463. A woman tourist in Greece rented a car and drove out to one of the ancient temples crumbling under the centuries. Posing near one huge fallen column, she asked a fellow tourist to take a snapshot.

"Don't get the car in the picture," she said, "or my husband will think I knocked this place down."

464. A man appeared in a newspaper office to place an ad offering $100 for the return of his wife's cat.

"That's an awfully high price for a cat," the clerk suggested.

"Not for this one," said the man. "I drowned it."

465. *Wife:* "I've got you this bottle of hair renewal, darling."

Husband: "But my hair isn't falling out."

Wife: "I know, but I want you to give it to your typist at the office; her hair is coming out rather badly."

466. *Housewife:* "Do you mind escorting me out to the garbage can, dear?"

Husband: "Why that?"

Wife: "I want to be able to tell the neighbors that we go out together once in a while."

467. Johnny's teacher wrote to his mother: "Johnny is a bright boy, but he seems to spend all his time thinking about girls."

Johnny's mother wrote back to his teacher: "If you find a cure, let me know. I'm having the same trouble with his father."

468. "How'd you come out in that fight with your wife?"
"She came crawling to me on her hands and knees."
"Yeah? What did she say?"
"Come out from under that bed, you coward!"

469. "You know, dear," he said breaking the long silence. "I've been thinking over our argument."
"Well," she snapped, without looking up from her reading.
"Yes, dear, I've decided to agree with you after all," he said meekly.
"That won't do you any good," she sniffed. "I've changed my mind."

470. A fellow came into a bar and ordered a martini. Before drinking it, he removed the olive and carefully put it into a glass jar. Then he ordered another martini and did the same thing. After an hour, when he was full of martinis and the jar was full of olives, he staggered out.
"Well," said a customer. "I never saw anything as peculiar as that!"
"What's so peculiar about it?" the bartender said. "His wife sent him out for a jar of olives."

471. *Husband in movie:* "Can you see, dear?"
Wife: "Yes."
Hubby: "Is there a draft on you?"
Wife: "No."
Husband: "Is your seat comfortable?"
Wife: "Yes."
Husband: "Let's change seats."

472. A widow recently married to a widower was accosted by a friend who laughingly remarked: "I suppose, like all men who have been married before, your husband sometimes talks about his first wife?"
"Oh, not any more, he doesn't," the other replied.
"What stopped him?"
"I started talking about my next husband."

473.   There are three kinds of spouses. Those you cannot live without, those you cannot live with—and those we live with.

474.   "Your mother has been living with us for five years now," said Sam. "Don't you think it's time she gets out on her own and makes a life for herself?"

"My mother?" questioned Mary. "I thought she was your mother."

475.   The proud new parents were strolling their new baby through the park when a lady of grandmother status commented, "Oh, he is adorable. What a cutie! How old is he?"

The father quickly responded, "Well, thank you. I just turned twenty-nine."

476.   Following a holiday of marathon football games on television, a wife attempted to wake her husband: "Honey, it's 10 to 7."

"Who's ahead?" he asked.

I

Identification—Identity

477. How to identify a car owner: He's the one who—after you pull the door shut—always opens it again and slams it harder.

478. Mrs. Trent, seated in her living room, heard the back door slam. Thinking it was her young son, she called: "I'm in here, darling. I've been waiting for you."

There was no answer for a moment. Then a strange voice faltered: "I'm sorry, but I ain't your regular milk deliverer."

479. Artist Pablo Picasso surprised a burglar at work in his new chateau. The intruder got away, but Picasso told the police he could do a rough sketch of what he looked like. On the basis of his drawing, the police arrested a mother superior, the minister of finance, a washing machine, and the Eiffel tower.

480. "My, how you've changed. You used to have thick, black hair and now you're bald. You used to have a florid complexion, and now you're pale. You used to be chunky, and now you're skinny. I'm really surprised at your change, Mr. Jones."

"But I'm not Mr. Jones."

"Heavens! You mean to say you've changed your name, too?"

481. Two lawyers were arguing a case in court and began to call each other names.

"You're a loop-brained shyster," roared one.

"And you're an ambulance-chasing cockroach," roared the other.

The judge finally rapped for order. "Now that you two have introduced each other to this court," he said, "you may proceed with the case."

482.   John Smith witnessed a minor holdup. In due time police arrived, and one officer asked the witness his name.

"John Smith," said Smith.

"Cut the comedy," snapped the cop. "What's your name?"

"All right," said Smith, "put me down as Winston Churchill."

"That's more like it," said the officer. "You can't pull that John Smith stuff on me!"

483.   Harold Hoffman, one-time governor of New Jersey, was an excellent storyteller. He used to swear this one happened:

A long-term state employee was driving a truck along a New Jersey highway and was exceeding the speed limit. A trooper flagged him down and said: "Do you realize you were doing fifty-five miles an hour?"

"No, I didn't," said the man.

"Haven't you a governor on that truck?"

"No, sir," said the employee, "the governor's in Trenton—that's fertilizer you smell."

484.   A legislative committee was assigned to investigate conditions in a mental hospital in an eastern state. There was a dance the evening of the day the committee arrived, and the members were invited to attend.

During the course of the dance, a legislative member took for his partner a pretty patient, to whom he had been introduced by a supervisor. "I don't remember having seen you before," she inquired. "How long have you been a patient here?"

"Oh, I'm not a patient," said the legislator. "I'm a member of a special legislative committee which came down here today to investigate the hospital."

"Of course," returned the lady patient. "How stupid of me. However, I knew the moment I saw you, you were either a member of the legislature or an inmate, and for the life of me I couldn't figure out which."

Ignorance

485.   An elderly lady and a young man were the only two passengers to leave the New York subway train at that station. The young man with his quick, long stride reached the exit gate long before the less agile woman. But there he stood, patiently holding the gate open for her. Upon reaching the gate, the lady smiled appreciatively and said, "Thank you so much. I'm really not accustomed to such good manners here in New York."

The young man tipped his hat courteously and replied, "You'll have to excuse me, ma'am. I'm from out of town myself and don't know any better."

486.   Learned counsel was addressing a judge who was obviously extremely hostile to the cause being pleaded. Nevertheless, counsel persisted in his argument, which was long and involved and highly technical. The judge heard him out with not very good grace, and when he had concluded could not resist saying, sneeringly: "Mr. Prodder has spoken at great length and with a good deal of eloquence, and I know it must pain him when I say that I, for one, have been left as ignorant as ever." Quick as a flash, counsel was on his feet and retorting: "Ignorant—yes, but surely a good deal better informed."

Illusion

487.   "Miss Henderson," said the boss, "I want you to prepare a statement for the press announcing that beginning March first this company will pay a pension of $300 a month to all employees who have been with us 20 years or longer."

"But, Mr. Allmant, this company has been in business for less than six months!"

"I know, but it'll look good in the papers anyhow."

488.   A young, struggling American sculptor went to study art in Paris. Like most students he had a hard time making ends meet. When winter came, his studio was bitterly cold, but since he was unable to pay his gas bill, he had to rely on his imagination to keep him warm.

He would place a lighted candle in the stove and cover the

door with a strip of red isinglass. The rosy glow gave such an illusion of warmth that he was able to continue his work without too much discomfort.

Illustration

489. *Judge:* "It is utterly incomprehensible to me how you could kill the man with one blow of your bare fist!"
Accused: "Shall I show you how I did it?"

490. A physician who was asked the difference between rheumatism and gout, answered: "If you take a vise, put a finger between, and turn until you can't stand it any longer, that's rheumatism; if you turn once more, that's gout."

Imitation

491. Little Herbert had bought Grandma a book for her birthday and wanted to write a suitable inscription on the flyleaf. He racked his brain until suddenly he remembered that his father had a book with an inscription of which he was very proud, so Herbie decided to use it.

You can imagine Grandma's surprise when she opened her book, a Bible, and found neatly inscribed the following phrase: "To Grandma, with the compliments of the author."

492. A man had a Chinese plate he valued very much. One day it fell and cracked down the middle. He ordered six more made and to insure the exact pattern, he sent his broken plate as a copy. When he received the package from China six months later, he was astonished to find the Chinese crafter had so faithfully followed his copy that each new plate had a crack right down the middle.

Moral: If we imitate even the best of people, we are bound to follow some of their imperfections.

Impatience

493. There is the story of the Sunday school teacher who asked a little boy if he knew where God's home was, confidently expecting that he would answer: "In heaven."

"In the bathroom at my house," replied the child.

"Why do you say that?" inquired the shocked teacher.

"Because every morning my daddy pounds on the door and says, 'My lord, are you still there?'"

494.   A wealthy manufacturer of 72 married an 18-year-old model. They honeymooned in Miami. After the honeymoon the manufacturer came down with a coronary. He was hospitalized and placed in an oxygen tent. His 18-year-old wife came to visit him.

When he saw her, the manufacturer began to speak. "Darling," he said, "I don't want you to worry about the future. My will has been made. You're going to get all my stocks and bonds, our house in Larchmont, the three cars, the property in Chicago, the villa in Monte Carlo, and a million-dollar trust fund."

Tears welled up in the wife's eyes. "Oh! Fred," she mumbled. "You've been so sweet to me, so kind. Tell me, husband dear, isn't there something I can do for you?"

"Yes," said the husband. "Take your finger away from the opening and let some oxygen into the tent."

Inadequacy

495.   Two cows were grazing alongside a highway when a tank-truck of milk on its way to the distributor happened to pass by. On one side of the truck in big red letters was a sign which read, "Pasteurized, homogenized, standardized, Vitamin A added."

One cow turned to the other and remarked, "Makes you feel sort of inadequate, doesn't it?"

Income Tax

496.   An income tax form is like a laundry list—either way you lose your shirt.

497.   The taxpayer no longer fears that Congress will let him down; he just hopes it will let him up.

498.   We aren't certain who thought up a tax deduction for children, but they must have been single.

499. America is the only country where it takes more brains to make out the income tax return than it does to make the income.

500. An Internal Revenue agent is writing a book called, *"How We Made $1,800,000 off the Person Who Wrote a Book About Making $2,000,000 in the Stock Market."*

501. "Look," said the business owner to her accountant. "Let's stop all those tricks. I want to pay my income tax in one lump."

"But you are permitted by law to pay it quarterly," the accountant explained.

"I know that," the boss replied. "But my heart can't take it four times a year."

502. Two income tax collectors died and arrived at the pearly gates. Just ahead of them were two clergy, but St. Peter motioned them aside and took the internal revenuers into heaven at once.

"Why them ahead of us?" the surprised religious leaders asked. "Haven't we done everything possible to spread the good word?"

"Yes," said St. Peter, "but those two internal revenue agents scared hell out of more people than you ever did."

Inflation

503. A few more years and a dollar-pincher will mean the same thing that a penny-pincher meant a generation ago.

504. Two shoppers in the supermarket were discussing inflation. The first woman remarked, "At least it has one point in its favor."

"Just what can be good about inflation?" asked the other.

"Well, these days it is almost impossible for the kids to get sick on a 50-cent candy bar."

Ingenuity

505. It happened somewhere in Massachusetts. The townspeople tried everything to get motorists to drive slow through a certain residential area. They posted signs such as "Please Drive Carefully," "Slow Down," and "Children at Play" . . . but to no avail. Nothing they did seemed to work—until they constructed a sign that read, "Nudist Colony Ahead."

Installment purchase

506. A sign in the gift shop read, "For the woman who has everything: a calendar to remind her when the payments are due."

507. "You pay a small deposit," said the salesperson, "and then make no more payments for six months."
"Who told you about us?" demanded the potential customer.

508. Have you heard the one about the farmer who walked into the dealer's showroom with a shoebox full of hundred dollar bills and tried to buy a tractor? The salesperson could tell him the monthly payments but he didn't know the cash price. The bookkeeper quit because she didn't know how to record the transaction, and the sales manager cancelled the sale because he didn't have a credit report.

Insurance

509. Some weeks after receiving a $1,200 check for the loss of her jewelry, an elderly woman informed her insurance company that she had found the missing property in her cupboard.
"I didn't think it would be fair to keep both the jewels and the money, so I think you will be pleased to know that I sent the $1,200 to the Red Cross."

510. Two vacationing businesspeople were comparing notes on the beach at Miami. One said, "I'm here on the insurance money I collected—got $50,000 for fire damage."
"Me, too," the second merchant said. "But I got $100,000 for flood damage."
There was a long thoughtful pause and then the first person said, "Tell me, how do you start a flood?"

511. The man informed the insurance agent that he wished to have his life insured.

"Do you drive a car?" asked the agent.

"No," replied the man.

"Do you often ride in buses or taxis?"

"No."

"Do you fly much?"

"No."

"Well, I'm very sorry, sir," the agent said firmly, "but we don't insure pedestrians."

Integrity

512. *Father (looking over report card) to small boy:* "One thing in your favor—with these grades, you couldn't possibly be cheating."

513. "My grocer gave me a phony quarter this morning. You can't trust anyone these days."

"Let's see it."

"I can't. I passed it at the drug store."

Intelligence

514. Five Americans, including the President, a minister, college student, the president of the National Mensa Society, and a pilot are flying in an airplane across the Atlantic.

Suddenly, the pilot emerges from the cockpit with four parachutes. As he straps one on, he says, "We've developed mechanical difficulties and we're going to crash." He tosses the remaining three parachute packs on the floor and jumps out of the airplane.

Immediately, the President stands up and says that since he is the leader of the country, he should parachute to save his life. The others agree and he jumps from the plane.

The Mensa Society president says, "Since I am the leader of America's most intelligent people, I can do much to better the world for everyone. I deserve a parachute. Before the others could mutter a word, she jumps from the plane.

The minister immediately speaks up: "My friend, you are

young and have a full life of learning and experience ahead of you. I, on the other hand, have enjoyed a full life and I am now ready to die and meet my maker. I want you . . ."

The student interrupts the minister, "Relax, pastor. We can both have a parachute. One of the most intelligent people in the world just jumped out of this airplane with my backpack."

Interpretation

515. It was Sunday morning. He slipped into his wife's dressing-gown and went downstairs to answer the door bell. As he opened the door, the milkman kissed him.

After giving due consideration to this unusual occurrence, he came to the conclusion that the milkman's wife must have a similar dressing-gown.

516. A dignitary, visiting Africa, made an appearance before a large gathering of natives. He launched into a long, rambling anecdote that went on for the better part of a half hour. The natives were respectfully silent.

When he had concluded, his interpreter rose and said four words. Everyone laughed uproariously.

The dignitary was stunned. "How could you tell my story so quickly?" he gasped.

"Story too long," said the interpreter. "So I say—'He tell joke. Laugh.' "

Introduction of speaker

517. *Chairperson:* "I never saw our speaker before tonight. If she's good, let's hear her. If she's not, let's get it over with."

518. For fully fifteen minutes an overbearing Washington toastmaster extolled the virtues of a popular Senator. It was becoming embarrassing. Just as the toastmaster paused to grasp for a few more phrases to end his introduction, the Senator's wife leaned over to her husband and in a voice that was louder than she intended it to be, remarked: "Hello, God!"

The toastmaster folded in a wave of laughter.

Invention—Inventions

519. How come, if necessity is the mother of invention, so much unnecessary stuff gets invented?

520. A Southern Senior Senator, voting against a bill to aid education, argued that the whole thing is a waste. "Science makes it impractical," he said. "Why, I once spent two years learnin' how to read; then they invented talkin' pictures and made the whole thing unnecessary."

J

Joint effort

521. Two moving men were struggling with a big crate in a doorway. They pushed and tugged until they were exhausted but it wouldn't move. Finally, the man on the outside said, "We'd better give up, we'll never get this in."

The fellow on the inside said, "What do you mean get it in? I thought you were trying to get it out."

522. Several years ago a musician was giving a brilliant concert in a famous old church. As he reached the intermission, he departed in back of the organ for a bit of rest. There he found an oldish gentleman smoking his pipe as he rested from the chore of pumping air for the big organ. The fellow smiled and commented: "We're giving them quite a concert, aren't we?"

This seemed out of perspective to the genius, who put the fellow in his place: "What do you mean 'we', old man? I'm giving the concert!"

He went out front. In came the audience, he struck the pose with hands raised and let them descend for the next number. There was no sound. He dashed behind the organ. There was the man, smoking his pipe. It dawned on the genius and with a smile he admitted: "You were right, we are giving them a concert."

Journalism

523. *Daughter:* "Daddy, why do all the editors refer to themselves as 'we'?"

Daddy: "So the reader who doesn't like what is printed, will think there are too many for him or her to lick."

524. "Could you give me some pointers," queried the journalism student, "on how to run a newspaper?"

"You came to the wrong person," answered the editor. "Ask one of my subscribers."

525. The city editor had just been informed that a wire had fallen across Main Street in a storm. She assigned two reporters to the story.

"No one knows whether the wire is live or not," she said. "So one of you is to touch it and the other to write the story."

526. "What," yelled the city editor as the cub reporter came in empty-handed. "You say there was no story in that big society wedding?"

"Not a word," mourned the cub. "The groom failed to show up."

527. *Film star:* "I told the newspapers that what I wanted most was a little cottage with a husband and at least six children."

Friend: "Goodness, what makes you say such silly things?"

Film star: "The publicity department."

528. *Jones:* "In an Australian newspaper office once I saw over the editor's chair the motto, 'Today's paper lights tomorrow's fire.'"

Smith: "That is to induce a proper humility in the staff?"

Jones: "No, it is to encourage them to take a chance with a story."

529. "What do you mean," roared the politician, "by publicly insulting me in your old rag of a paper? I will not stand for it, and I demand an immediate apology."

"Just a moment," answered the editor. "Didn't the news appear exactly as you gave it to us—namely, that you had resigned as city treasurer?"

"It did, but where did you put it?—in the column under the heading *'Public Improvements.'*"

530. The editor looked over the proofs of the book on child care and decided that the author had used the word "underpants" too often.

So the editor jotted down a notation on his calendar pad to "change underpants" in order to remind the author of this change.

The next morning, the editor's private secretary scanned her boss' calendar, scratched her head and mumbled, "What will that guy want me to remind him of next!"

531. The young woman had just left journalism school and got a job on the staff of a local paper. She listened intently to the editor's instructions:

"Never write anything as a fact unless you are absolutely sure about it, or you'll get the paper into trouble. Make it a point to use the words, 'alleged', 'reputed', 'claimed', 'rumored', or 'it was said.'"

The youthful reporter kept repeating this instruction to herself as she went out on her first assignment, and this is her first story:

"It is rumored that a party was given yesterday by a number of reputed ladies. Mrs. Smith, it was said, was hostess, and the guests, it is alleged, with the exception of Mrs. Jones, who says she is fresh from London, were all local people. Mrs. Smith claims to be the wife of Joe Smith, rumored to be the president of an alleged bank."

Jurisdiction

532. Asked to officiate at a friend's wedding ceremony, a Supreme Court Justice member explained that he did not have the authority to perform the ceremony.

"What!" exclaimed his friend. "A Supreme Court Justice doesn't have the authority to marry people! How come?"

"I guess," replied the Supreme Court Justice, "it is because marriage is not considered a federal offense."

Justice

533. They had been married just two weeks and he was going through a batch of mail that had arrived that morning.

"Honey," he said, "aren't these bills for the clothes you bought before we were married?"

"Yes, darling," she replied. "You're not upset about it, are you?"

"Well," he retorted, "don't you think it's unfair to ask a fish to pay for the bait he was caught with?"

534. Two police magistrates were driving home together at night, when they were stopped by a motorcycle police officer. They were duly charged and, when their cases came up for hearing the next day, they agreed that each should leave the bench in turn to have his case heard by the other.

The first went to trial, pleaded guilty and was promptly fined twenty-five dollars and costs. When they changed places the second magistrate, after pleading guilty, was rather shocked to receive a fine of fifty dollars and costs.

"That's a bit unfair," he complained. "I only fined you twenty-five dollars."

"I know," was the reply, "but there is too much of this sort of thing going on—this is the second case we've had today."

K

Kindness

535. The teacher had asked her small pupils to tell about their acts of kindness to dumb animals. After several heart-stirring stories, the teacher asked Tommy if he had anything to add. "Well," he replied rather proudly, "I kicked a boy once for kicking his dog."

Kiss—Kisses—Kissing

536. *She:* "I'm telling you for the last time that I won't let you kiss me!"
He: "I knew you'd weaken!"

537. The young artist kissed his model smack on the lips.
"I'll bet you do that to all your models," she said when she had regained her composure.
"No," he replied, "you are the first."
"How many have you had?" she inquired.
"Exactly four," he answered. "A rose, an onion, a banana, and you."

Know-how

538. The history class was studying the Revolutionary battle of Saratoga which was probably lost because General William Howe chose to remain in Philadelphia. The teacher then asked the class to explain this major British defeat.
"Lack of no Howe," answered a voice from the back of the classroom.

539. It is said that Emerson visited a farm one day and was amused to see a boy from a nearby city trying to put a calf into a barn. He shoved and the calf shoved. When he pulled, the calf pulled the other way. A farm girl, standing nearby, smiled, walked over and put her middle finger into the calf's mouth and gently led it into the barn.

540. A little girl returned from her first day in school and proudly exclaimed, "Mother, I was the brightest one in my class!"

"That's fine, Janie," her mother said, "but tell me how it happened."

"Well," Janie replied, "the teacher told each one of us to draw a picture on the blackboard, and then the others were to guess what the picture was. Mine was the only one no one could guess— but I knew exactly what it was all the time!"

L

Landlord—Tenant

541.   Give people an inch these days and they will rent it.

542.   A group of American tourists were being guided through an ancient castle in Europe.

"This place," the guide told them, "is 600 years old. Not a stone in it has been touched, nothing altered, nothing replaced in all those years."

"Well," said one woman dryly, "they must have the same landlord I have."

Language

543.   The visiting American and his English friend were driving through London when the latter mentioned that his windscreen needed cleaning. "Windshield," the American corrected him.

"Well, over here we call it a windscreen."

"Then you're wrong," argued the American. "After all, we Americans invented the automobile, and we call this a windshield."

"That's all very well, old boy," snapped the Englishman, "but who invented the language?"

Laughter

544.   Laugh and the world laughs with you. Cry and you may not cry alone, but you'll never get a group discount.
Estrucan Philosopher

545. . . . he never knew a man who possessed the gift of hearty laughter to be burdened by constipation. I can readily agree with him.

Norman Cousins

546. It's bad to suppress laughter. It goes back down and spreads your hips.

Fred Allen

547. If there is nothing to laugh about, laugh on credit.

548. An onion can make people cry, but there has never been a vegetable invented to make them laugh.

Will Rogers

549. Professional comedian and singer Eddie Cantor conducted a benefit performance at a veteran's hospital. He gave every song his best and worked hard to make the patients laugh. Closing the show, he commented, "Hope you're all better soon."

His audience of veterans simultaneously responded, "Same to you."

Lawyer—Lawyers

550. Did you hear about the lawyer's daughter who told her boyfriend, "Stop, and/or I'll slap your face"?

551. One night when the family was around the dinner table, Alan looked at his mother very seriously and asked:

"Mommy, when are you going to stop practicing law and really do it?"

552. Once upon a time the fence between heaven and hell broke down. St. Peter appeared at the broken section and called out to the devil: "Hey, Satan, since all the engineers are over in your place, how about getting them to fix this fence?"

"Sorry," replied Satan. "My men are all too busy to go about fixing measly fences."

"Well, then," replied St. Peter, "I'll have to sue you if you don't."

"Oh, yeah," countered the devil, "and where are you going to get a lawyer?"

553. Professor of Law Samuel Siegel helped would-be attorneys understand how to tackle difficult cases. "When you're presenting a case, if you have the facts on your side, hammer the facts," Siegel advised. "If you have the law on your side, then hammer the law."

"What if you don't have the facts or the law," a student asked, "then what do you do?"

"Well, in that case," responded Siegel, "hammer on the table."

Lawyer—Client

554. *Lawyer (over telephone)*: "They can't put you in jail for that."

Client: "Oh, yeah? Where do you think I'm phoning from—the public library?"

555. "You're a cheat!" shouted the lawyer's client. "You're a blackguard! You've kept me hanging for months and got rich on my case alone!"

"That's gratitude!" said the aggrieved lawyer sadly. "And right after I named my new yacht after you!"

556. A wealthy financier laid a case before his attorney. When he had finished, the lawyer was enthusiastic. "It's an iron-clad case," he said confidently. "We can't possibly lose!"

"I guess we won't sue then," said the financier. "That was my opponent's side of the case I gave you."

557. *Judge:* "You wish your trial postponed because your counsel has been taken ill; but since you were caught red-handed and have confessed the theft, I don't see what your counsel could say in your favor."

Prisoner: "That's just what I am curious to hear, your Honor!"

558. A woman charged with theft showed up in court without an attorney.

"Do you want me to assign you an attorney?" asked the presiding judge.

"No, sir," said the defendant.

"But you are entitled to an attorney and you might as well have the benefit of legal services," said the portly jurist.

"If it's all the same with you," said the defendant, "I'd like to throw myself upon the ignorance of the court."

559.   A new lawyer had just opened up his office. "Ah! A client already," he thought as he saw the door opening. "I must impress him."

He picked up the telephone. "No, I'm very sorry, but I can't take your case, even for $1,000," he said. "I'm just too busy."

He replaced the receiver and looked at his caller. "And now, what can I do for you?" he asked briskly.

"Nothing, really," was the reply. "I just came to connect your telephone."

560.   The plaintiff in a damage suit had enjoyed very little education in his life and was wholly unused to court proceedings. He was considerably disturbed to see that the defendant corporation had two men from its legal staff on the case.

During the recess for lunch, he turned to his own lawyer and said, "I ought to have a second lawyer on my side."

"What's the matter?" demanded his astonished counsel. "I think I am presenting your case very effectively. In fact, I don't see how we can lose."

The plaintiff stroked his chin reflectively. Then he explained, "I notice the corporation has two lawyers. When one of them is up speakin' for their side, the other is sittin' there thinkin'. When you're up speakin' for our side, there ain't nobody thinkin'."

Laziness

561.   A famous trainer of racing thoroughbreds, was once asked how he happened to choose his career.

"When I was a boy on the farm," he explained, "I was wild about horses and cows. I knew I would spend my life raising one or the other."

"How did you decide which?"

"That was easy," said the trainer. "I didn't have to milk horses."

562. The sergeant looked disdainfully at the new recruits. "Men," he shouted, "I have a nice easy job for the laziest rookie here. Will the laziest man step forward?"

Instantly, all the men stepped forward—all but one.

"Why don't you step up to the front with the others?" demanded the sergeant.

"Too much trouble," drawled the rookie.

563. The patient explained to the doctor that he was unable to perform all the responsibilities on his job that he used to. The doctor ran a series of tests and questioned the patient for further details. When the examination was complete, the curious patient said, "Tell it to me straight, doctor. I can handle the results."

"Well, it is quite simple," the doctor replied, "you're just plain lazy."

"Okay, I can take that," said the man. "Now could you write down the medical term so I can give it to my supervisor?"

564. The business owner carefully observed a new employee for the first thirty days. Not being a real ball of fire, the employee displayed a less-than-enthusiastic work ethic. Unable to restrain herself any longer, the owner screamed, "You're one of the laziest people I have ever seen. You have barely completed a week's worth of work since I hired you. Help me understand one reason why I should keep you around?"

The employee calmly pondered the question and then responded, "One benefit is that when I take a vacation, you won't need to find someone to fill in."

Learning

565. A man and his young son were taking a bus trip. The boy kept his curious eyes glued out the window with his nose pressed against it. The sites along the way prompted questions from the young boy.

"What that truck hauling, Daddy?"

"I don't know," mumbled the father, engrossed in his newspaper.

"What makes it snow?"

"I can't answer that."

"How fast do airplanes fly?"

"Son, quit pestering me with all your questions!"

Another passenger, overhearing the little boy's questions, commented, "You sure do have a curious young lad."

"You bet," replied the father. "How else will he become as knowledgeable as his dad?"

Legacy—Legacies

566.   The will of the wealthy, but eccentric, man was being read and the relatives all listened expectantly, especially his less-than-responsible nephew. Finally the lawyer said, "And to my nephew, Charlie Jones, whom I promised to remember—'Hi, there, Charlie!"

567.   The head of a large mercantile company had died and his secretary had been notified that on reading his will they found she had been named as one of his beneficiaries.

"Oh, no," she said. "I thought all the time he had one, but it wasn't me, honest it wasn't."

568.   "This may be gossip, but I heard Jim Johnson married Sarah Doolittle just because her uncle left her a lot of money."

"Well, I've known Jim a long time, and you can tell 'em for me it ain't so. He would have married Sarah no matter who left her the money."

569.   When the will was read, all the relatives of the famous industrialist gathered to hear what he had left them. To his wife went most of the large estate, to some cousins went several thousand dollars, and to various others went lesser but substantial gifts.

"And lastly," read the lawyer, "to my nephew, Henry, who was always telling me that health is far more important to a person than wealth, I now leave the entire contents of my third floor closet—my exercise bike."

Lifestyle

570.   The important question is how long you should go without exercising before eating.

The Muppets Miss Piggy

571.   I know a man who gave up smoking, drinking, sex, and rich food. He was healthy right up to the time he killed himself.

Johnny Carson

572.   Be careful about reading health books. You may die of a misprint.

Mark Twain

573.   Some people confine their exercise to jumping to conclusions, running up bills, stretching the truth, bending over backward, lying down on the job, sidestepping responsibility, and pushing their luck.

Anonymous

Listening

574.   A prominent party hostess had her doubts that anybody really listened to each other at cocktail parties. To test her theory, the hostess conducted an unusual experiment. As she served hors d'oeuvres to guests, the hostess commented, "Do try this one. I've flavored them with strychnine."

The guests inhaled the goodies. Most commented, "Delicious!" "Very tasty!" Others mentioned the special flavoring while several requested the recipe for their next party.

575.   Archie Bunker to his wife Edith: "The reason you don't understand me is because I'm talkin' to you in English and you're listenin' in Dingbat."

576.   A Social Work student was learning the value of reflective listening—summarizing what someone has said to show you heard them accurately. At the conclusion of several practice sessions, each student was asked to choose someone with whom they could practice their new skills. Mary chose her eight-year-old neighbor boy.

"Hi Jimmy," she began. "How have things been going?"

"Not very good," Jimmy responded.

"You haven't been doing too good?" Mary questioned.

"No, I have been in trouble with my mom most of the week."

"You have been in trouble with your mom?"

"Ya, and it's not my fault."

"Not your fault?"

"Mary, you seem to have the same problem my mom tells me I have," Jimmy exclaimed. "It seems we both don't hear too well."

Life insurance. See Insurance

Longevity

577.   I can't die. I'm booked.

George Burns

578.   One way to live longer is to cut out all the things that make you want to live longer.

579.   A reporter, interviewing a woman who had reached her 99th birthday, said, "I certainly hope I can come back next year and see you reach 100."

"Can't see why not, young feller," the elderly woman replied, "you look healthy enough to me."

Long-windedness

580.   Some speakers are like some gamblers—they don't have sense enough to quit while they're ahead.

581.   "I am a person of few words," shouted a House member as he started his second hour of a gusty speech.

"That may well be," snickered a nearby colleague, "but you are keeping them mighty busy."

582.   An ambassador, on a mission to Sparta from Perinthus, overdid himself by speaking at great length. "What answer shall I give to the Perinthians?" the diplomat asked.

"You may say," replied the King, "that you talked a great deal—while I said nothing."

583.   While Adlai Stevenson was campaigning in California, a woman asked him where he got his coat of deep tan.

"You been playing golf?" she accused him.

"No," replied Adlai, "I got this tan making outdoor speeches in Florida."

"Well," the woman told him, "if you got that brown you talked too long."

Loquacity

584.   Talk about others and you're a gossip; talk about yourself and you're a bore.

585.   A senator was asked to comment about a talkative colleague: "When he gets started, his tongue is like a race horse; it runs fastest the less weight it carries."

Losing

586.   Homecoming was a disaster. The home team, celebrating their school's 50th homecoming football game, was easily defeated by a score of 73 to 14. The fans were unimpressed, the players were depressed, but the coach maintained his sense of humor. A reporter asked what he felt the turning point was. The coach hesitated a moment and then responded: "Somewhere between the time we left the locker room and the conclusion of the national anthem."

Luck

587.   David, a second-grader, was bumped while getting on the school bus and suffered a two-inch cut on his cheek. At recess he collided with another boy and two of his teeth were knocked loose. At noon while sliding on ice, he fell and broke his wrist. Later at the hospital, his father noticed David was clutching a quarter in his good hand. "I found it on the ground when I fell," David said. "This is the first quarter I ever found. This sure is my lucky day."

588. A grocer, while delivering orders in his station wagon, ran down and seriously injured an elderly lady. The lady sued and was awarded an amount large enough to drive the man out of business. After difficult times he managed to accumulate enough to try again. But a few months after opening his doors he struck an old gentleman with his delivery truck. The gentleman sued and collected big damages, enough to ruin him.

On a peaceful Sunday the grocer was sitting in his living room when his little boy entered and called out, "Father, Father, Mother's been run over by a great big bus."

The grocer's eyes filled with tears, and in a voice trembling with emotion he cried, "Thank the Lord, the luck's changed at last."

M

Man—Woman

589. About the only time a woman really succeeds in changing a male is when he's a baby.

590. A pompous gentleman once asked the sharp-tongued actress, Mrs. Patrick Campbell, "Why do you suppose it is that women so utterly lack a sense of humor?"

"God did it on purpose," Mrs. Campbell answered without batting an eyelash, "so that we may love you men instead of laughing at you."

Marriage

591. For every person who marries for money there's another who marries for alimony.

592. Some people marry poor to settle down, and others marry rich to settle up.

593. Marriage is like a violin. After the beautiful music is over, the strings are still attached.

594. Marriages may be made in heaven, but a lot of the details have to be worked out here on earth.

595. One good reason why a man should get married: He doesn't have to blame everything on the government.

596. *She:* "Before we got married, you told me you were well off."

He: "I was and I didn't know it."

597. Marriage would work out better if both sides would operate not only on a fifty-fifty basis but on a thrifty-thrifty basis as well.

598. Two old codgers were chatting on a park bench. Said one to the other: "If they'd have had electric blankets and sliced bread when I was a lad, I'd never have got married."

599. A shoe repair sign advertised a leading brand of rubber heel with a lovely lady remarking, "I'm in love with America's Number One Heel." Under this, in a feminine hand, someone added, "Sorry, sister, I married him!"

600. Recently a Canadian newspaper received this anxious epistle from one of its readers: "I read with trepidation that the Church of England is omitting the word 'obey' from the marriage service in their new prayer book. May I ask if this new church law is retroactive?"

601. After the hillbilly wedding one of the local citizens approached the bride's father and said:
"Hey, Zeke, your son-in-law marched up to the altar as though he had lead in his pants!"
Zeke shifted his chaw of tobacco, spat out of the side of his mouth and replied: "He did."

602. A citizen of ancient Rome sought to divorce her husband, and as a result was severely chastened by her friends, who asked: "Was he not chaste? Was he not fair?"
The Roman held out one of her shoes. "Is it not well made?" She said. "Is it not also new?" And when they had agreed that the shoe was both well made and new, the Roman replied: "Yet none of you can tell where it pinches me."

603. Mark Twain once debated the question of polygamy with a Mormon acquaintance. The discussion became heated, and finally the Mormon resorted to the Bible for his affirmative clincher. "Can you tell me of a single passage of Scripture wherein polygamy is forbidden?"
"Certainly," Twain replied. "No man can serve two masters."

604.   He confided to his old friend that life was now empty because, "The woman I love has just refused my proposal of marriage."

"Well, don't let that get you down," comforted the friend. "A woman's 'no' often means 'yes'."

"She didn't say 'no'," came the dejected reply. "She said 'phooey'."

605.   A young bride-and-groom-to-be had just selected the wedding ring. As the girl admired the plain platinum and diamond band, she suddenly looked concerned. "Tell me," she asked the elderly salesperson, "is there anything special I'll have to do to take care of this ring?"

With a fatherly smile, the salesperson said: "One of the best ways to protect a wedding ring is to dip it in dishwater three times a day."

606.   Shortly after completing his training, a young counselor was asked to speak at a young couples club on marital sex. When his wife asked about the topic of his speech that night, he mumbled the first thing that came to his mind—sailing. Later in the week at the grocery store, a friend came up to the wife and said how much the couple's club enjoyed the speech. "Really," the wife replied. "Frankly, I'm somewhat surprised. He's only tried it a few times. Once he got sick and the other time his hat blew off."

607.   Did you hear about the guy, who after a delicious dinner, walked over to his wife, leaned over, and whispered in her ear: "That was a great dinner sweetheart. I love you."

The wife quickly rose without saying a word, went over, and recorded the event in her pocket calendar.

608.   Some spouses act as if they're training for congress, the way they're always bringing new bills to the house.
                      Los Angeles Times Syndicate

609.   When one beautiful woman asked another why a girl of her age and talents would marry a wealthy old man, she replied:

"Listen, if anyone offered you a check for $1,000,000, would you stop to look at the date?"

Married life. See also Husband—Wife

610. The story of some marriages should be told in a scrapbook.

611. Some people wonder how they could live without their spouse. The answer is, cheaper.

612. The hostess was pressing her guests to provide entertainment. "Is there any instrument you can play, Mrs. Jones?"
"Not away from home," she replied.
"What do you play at home?" she inquired.
"Second fiddle," Jones muttered solemnly.

613. Into a Chicago club walked a member wearing an unaccustomed coat of tan on his cheeks and forehead.
"Hello, there," called one of his fellow club members. "Been sailing or did you get that on the beach?"
"Neither," came the reply. "I took my vacation at home. You see, our kitchen sink faces south."

614. Sitting silently at the bar, the woman sipped her drink, while on her face was an expression of extreme sadness.
"Mary," asked a friend, "what in the world is the matter?"
"Oh, I'm having troubles with my husband," Mary explained.
"What happened?"
"Well, he told me he wasn't going to speak to me for thirty days."
"But," her friend objected, "that ought to make you happy."
"It did," Mary answered, "but today is the last day."

Medical profession

615. A nurse in the maternity ward asked a young medical student why he was so enthusiastic about obstetrics. He said sheepishly, "When I was on medical rotation I suffered from heart attacks, asthma and itch. In surgery I was sure I had ulcers. In the psychiatric wards I thought I was losing my mind. Now, in obstetrics I can relax."

616. A doctor had trouble with his plumbing. The pipes in his bathroom began to leak. The leak became bigger and bigger.

Even though it was 2 a.m., the doctor decided to phone his plumber. Naturally the plumber got sore being awakened at that hour of the morning. "For Pete's sake, Doc," he wailed. "This is some time to wake up a guy."

"Well," the doctor answered testily, "you've never hesitated to call me in the middle of the night with a medical problem. Now, it just happens I've got a plumbing emergency."

There was a moment's silence. Then the plumber spoke up. "Right you are, Doc," he agreed. "Tell me what's wrong."

The doctor explained about the leak in the bathroom.

"Tell you what to do," the plumber offered. "Take two aspirins every four hours, drop them down the pipe. If the leak hasn't cleared up by morning, phone me at the office."

Medication

617. The trouble with not taking some kind of pills is that your associates will think you're overconfident.

Membership, Club. See Club membership

Mind, Presence of

618. One of the most tactful speeches ever thought up suddenly was spoken by the man who blundered into a bathroom where a woman was bathing and calmly turned and left with the words, "I beg your pardon—sir."

619. During Navy maneuvers, the captain was pushing his destroyer to the limit when a sailor came to the bridge with a message from the admiral. "Read it aloud," beamed the captain.

"Of all the blundering idiots. You nearly rammed the flagship," he read.

The captain pursed his lips, then snapped, "Very well, sailor, go below and have it decoded."

620. An Army driver was chauffeur to a major who was a notorious wolf.

One day, the major saw a lovely girl. "Turn the car round," he ordered. The driver promptly stalled the car.

By the time he had re-started it, the girl had vanished.

"Driver," said the major, "you'd be a total loss in an emergency!"

"I thought I did pretty well," the driver said. "That was my girl."

621.   The toastmaster was seated between two distinguished United States senators at a big New York dinner. He rose, and in complimentary language, declared: "Ladies and gentlemen, it is my very high privilege to present to you an old friend; a man who is a staunch supporter of the Constitution. He is regarded in Washington as a friend of the veteran, a friend of business and of labor, a brilliant lawmaker. May I present to you at this time, the Honorable . . . the Honorable . . ."

Here the toastmaster became bewildered. Then, turning quickly from one senator to the other, he sputtered, with a broad flush:

"By the way, which one of you wants to speak first?"

622.   A film director had been on location for two weeks and in the course of making the picture had fallen head-over-heels in love with the leading lady. Upon his return, rumors of the affair had reached the director's wife.

On the night of his homecoming, they retired. The director dropped off to sleep, and soon was talking in his slumbers: "Darling, you know I love you. You're more to me than anything else on earth."

Suddenly, he awakened, glanced at his wife's hostile face, and sensed the situation. Immediately he turned over, pretended he was still asleep, and remarked: "Cut! Now bring in the horses."

623.   A persistent party member once appeared before President Lincoln and demanded appointment to a judgeship as reward for some campaigning he'd done in Illinois. The President, aware of the man's lack of judicial attributes, told him it was impossible. "There simply are no vacancies at the present time," Mr. Lincoln said.

The man left. Early the next morning he was walking along the Potomac when he saw a drowned man pulled from the river and immediately recognized him as a federal judge. Without a moment of hesitation he presented himself to Mr. Lincoln while the President was eating breakfast, told him what he had seen, and demanded an immediate appointment to the vacancy.

Lincoln shook his head. "I'm sorry, sir, but you came too late," said the President. "I have already appointed the lawyer who saw him fall in."

Mistake—Mistakes

624.   A group of ministers and a sales organization were holding conventions in the same hotel. The catering department had to work at top speed serving dinners to both. The sales people were having "Spiked Watermelon" for dessert. But the harassed chef discovered this alcoholic tidbit was being served to the ministers by mistake. "Quick," he commanded a waiter. "If they haven't eaten the watermelon, bring it back and we'll give it to the sales people."

The waiter returned in a minute and reported it was too late—the ministers were eating the liquor-spiced dessert.

"Well," demanded the excited chef. "What did they say? How did they like it?"

"I don't know how they liked it," replied the waiter, "but they were dividing up the seeds and putting them in their pockets."

625.   Germany's late Cardinal von Faulhaber of Munich once had a conversation with the renowned mathematician, Albert Einstein.

"Cardinal von Faulhaber," Einstein remarked. "I respect religion, but I believe in mathematics. Probably it is the other way around with you."

"You are mistaken," the Cardinal retorted. "To me, both are merely different expressions of the same divine exactness."

"But, Your Eminence, what would you say if mathematical science should some day come to conclusions directly contradictory to religious beliefs?"

"Oh," answered the Cardinal, "I have the highest regard for

the competence of mathematicians. I am sure they would never rest until they discovered their mistake."

626.   Following his vote on a famous compensation bill, a senator found a formidable opposition arrayed against him for re-election. After addressing a crowd, he was stepping down from the platform to mingle with the voters when he was approached by an old friend named Scott—a great hunter and voter in his district.

"Well, Henry," said Scott, "I've been with you in six troubles, and I'm sorry I must desert you in the seventh. You voted for that miserable compensation bill and now I must turn my back on you."

"Is that your only objection?" asked the senator.

"It is."

"You are an avid hunter," said the senator, "and have killed many a fat bear and buck?"

"Yes," said Scott.

"I believe you have a good rifle?" the senator continued.

"Yes, as good a one as ever cracked."

"Well, then, did you ever have a fine buck before you when your gun misfired?"

"Yes, that has happened."

"Well, now, friend Scott, did you take that faithful rifle and break it to pieces on the very next log just because it misfired once, or did you reload and try again?"

"No, sir," laughed Scott. "I reloaded and tried again. And I'll try you again. Give me your hand."

The crowd also got the point, the story spread, and the senator was re-elected.

627.   The women's basketball coach at the University of Maine reflected on his team's 115-57 loss to Virginia. "I think the whole game hinged on a single call," he said.

"Which call was that?" asked a sports writer.

"The one I made last April scheduling the game."

628.   A young vice-president was appointed by the board of a bank to replace the retiring president and founder. With fear and trepidation, he made an appointment to visit with the grouchy retiree to seek his advice.

"Mr. Clark, I need your counsel. How can I possibly be successful in your old job?"

The elderly man looked over the top of his wire rim glasses. "Young man," he growled, "these two words are the key to your success—RIGHT DECISIONS!"

"Thank you, sir. But how can I make sure I am making right decisions?"

"EXPERIENCE. Experience will insure you make right decisions."

A long silence followed. "That is helpful," said the young man, "but how do I get the right experience?"

The elderly man stood, grasping the hand of the aspiring executive, he looked him directly in the eye, smiled, and responded, "WRONG DECISIONS."

629. A professional carpet-layer stepped back to admire his customary flawless work. While surveying the installed carpet, he reached into his shirt pocket for a cigarette and realized they were missing. At the same time, he noted a lump under the carpet, about the size of a cigarette package. Frustrated with his carelessness, the carpet layer realized he was in a predicament. There was no way to retrieve his cigarette package from under the attached carpet. Finally, he decided to beat the object flat, thereby destroying any evidence of his mistake.

Satisfied with the outcome, he picked up his tools and began loading the truck. He couldn't believe his eyes. Laying on the seat of his truck was the mislaid pack of cigarettes. "But what about . . . ?" It was then that the homeowner's voice broke his disbelief.

"Hey, have you seen my son's gerbil?"

630. Don't make the wrong mistakes.
Yogi Berra

631. An avid fisher drove to northern Minnesota to do a little ice fishing. While attempting to drill a hole in the ice, he heard a voice from above declare, "There aren't any fish in there!"

The man moved his gear to another spot and began drilling. Again a voice from above said, "There aren't any fish in there."

The man dropped his gear, looked to the heavens, and asked, "Is that God speaking?"

The voice replied, "No, I'm the rink manager."

632. A fishing crew became marooned on a deserted island. For years they enjoyed each other's company but all three privately dreamed of being rescued and returning home. One day while fishing on the shoreline, a bottle washed up in front of them. A genie popped out and said, "It is my desire to grant you each your fondest wish."

"I know what I want," the first one quickly said, "I want to go home." His wish was granted—and poof!—home he went. "I want to go home, too," the second fisher said, and in a flash she was gone.

The third person pondered the alternatives. "I want to make sure I make the right decision, he said. "The last few years have been difficult but there has been value in being deserted on this island with Jerry and Sally. They are great people. I miss them already. Sure do wish they were here . . ."

Misunderstanding

633. Bill was taking an aptitude test to become an insurance salesperson. Everything was going good until question 21. It read: "How far is the earth from the moon?" Bill turned to the examiner and commented, "If you're expecting me to cover that territory, you can forget it!"

634. A traveling salesperson was dining at his favorite restaurant chain. However, the usual steak ordered well done was served in rare condition. Irritated, he furiously motioned for the waiter.

As the waiter approached his table, the salesperson blurted, "I said WELL DONE!"

"Well, thank you," responded the waiter, "your compliment is appreciated."

Modern Age

635. They're offering a new course in the more modern schools—stair climbing. It's for youngsters raised in ranch houses.

636. The modern college president has three important problems . . . salaries for the professors, football for the alumni and parking space for the students.

637. The modern home is going to be equipped with the latest in domestic kitchen appliances. You press a button and it lights the gas by rubbing two sticks together.

638. "Daddy, will you give me a dollar?"
"When I was your age, I asked for pennies."
"OK, give me 100 pennies."

639. A Brooklyn man took his wife to the Newark airport and put her on a plane for Buffalo. After fighting his way through the traffic, he arrived back home and wearily ascended the steps to his home to find a telegram in his mailbox. He opened it and read, "Arrived Safely. Love, Lulu."

640. Two business executives were watching a big excavation job being done by machinery. "If it wasn't for those machines," said one, "a thousand people might be using shovels."
"Yes," replied the other, "and if it wasn't for those shovels 1,000,000 people might be using teaspoons."

641. The junior executive had been complaining to his wife of aches and pains. Neither one could account for his trouble. Arriving home from work one night, he informed her, "I finally discovered why I've been feeling so miserable. We got some ultra-modern office furniture two weeks ago, and I just learned today that I've been sitting in the wastebasket."

642. A business firm wrote to another corporation, saying, "Our electronic brain has computed that the cost of the work you want done will be . . ."
The following reply was received a few days later:

"As this is more than we anticipated, we would like to suggest that your electronic brain make an appointment with our electronic brain to discuss ways and means of reducing the cost of work."

Money

643.   When I was a kid, I was so poor . . . that in my neighborhood, the rainbow was in black and white.
                                                    Rodney Dangerfield

644.   People are finding it increasingly difficult to support both the government and family on one salary.

Money Management

645.   Mother and Dad helped their oldest daughter pack her belongings and prepare for her first year of college. She was loaded with every conceivable item needed to begin an independent lifestyle including her very first checkbook. Within two months, bank overdrafts began arriving at the parents' home, all on their daughter's account.

"How are things at school?" Dad began his phone conversation.

"Just fine, Daddy," the coed responded.

"Mary," her dad admonished, "you've written over $300 in checks when there was only $10 left in your account. You are substantially overdrawn."

"But that can't be," argued Mary, "I still have checks left!"

Modern art. See Art, Modern

Mother-in-law

646.   Behind every successful person stands a devoted spouse—and a surprised mother-in-law.

647.   The modern couple usually gets along fine with their mother-in-law because they can't afford another baby sitter.

648.   Sometimes you can't tell if a person is trying so hard to be a success to please their spouse or to spite the mother-in-law.

649.   A newly-married man found his wife in tears when he arrived home from the office.

"You know the cake I made from mother's recipe?" she sobbed. "Well, I put it out to cool and the cat ate half of it."

"Never mind, darling," he comforted. "I know someone who will give us a kitten."

650.   A big game hunter went to Africa with his wife and his mother-in-law. They hired a guide who took them on a safari into the wilds of the jungle. One night, about a week after they were out, the husband and his wife awoke and discovered that mama was missing. After searching an hour for her, they were shocked to find her cowering in a clearing with a huge lion standing over her.

"Oh, what are we going to do?" the horrified wife asked.

"Nothing," answered the husband. "The lion got himself into that fix—now let him get out of it."

651.   The young wife was in tears when she opened the door for her husband. "I've been insulted," she sobbed. "Your mother insulted me."

"My mother!" he exclaimed. "But she is a hundred miles away."

"I know, but a letter came for you this morning and I opened it."

He looked stern. "I see, but where does the insult come in?"

"In the postscript," she answered. "It said: "Dear Alice, don't forget to give this letter to George.""

Music

652.   The village band finished a vigorous and not overharmonious selection. As the perspiring musicians sank to their seats after acknowledging the applause, the trombonist asked, "What's the next number?"

The leader replied, "The Washington Post March."

"Oh, no," gasped the trombonist. "I just got through playing that!"

653.   At a large party a Hollywood hostess decided to sing. In an off-pitch voice she rendered *Carry Me Back to Old Virginee*. She really belted the song, and as she sang, she noticed a distinguished, white-haired guest bow his head and weep quietly. When she finished the hostess approached the old man and said, "Pardon me, sir, but are you a Virginian?"

"No, ma'am," said the elderly guest, wiping away a tear. "I'm a musician."

N

Name—Names

654. "Does this package belong to you? The name is obliterated."

"Can't be mine. My name is Smith."

655. The manufacturer of a mobile outhouse for construction sites has hit upon an ideal name for it. He calls it Johnnie on the Spot.

656. *Assistant:* "Chief, there's an applicant who says he used to make his living by sticking his right arm into a lion's mouth."

Boss: "What's his name?"

Assistant: "Lefty."

657. It's the newspaper headline writers who really decide who will be president. To fit into headline space, names have to be reduced to three letters . . . FDR, HST, Ike, JFK . . . a poor guy named Stanford O. Buckley just wouldn't have a chance.

658. At a dinner party, two women had just been introduced to each other.

"Oh, yes," said one of them very sweetly. "We met two years ago at the Johnson's—I'm terribly bad at remembering names, but I never forget a dress."

659. A mother sat knitting one evening as her daughter was reading a book that gave the meaning of names. As the mother knitted she thought of all the young men who called on her daughter.

"Mother," her daughter remarked. "It says that Philip means 'Lover of Horses,' and James means 'Beloved'. I wonder what George means?"

"I hope dear," replied her mother, "in view of the alarming way that you and George have been carrying on, that George means business."

660. A teacher took over a new class: "What's your name?" she asked one little boy.

"Jule," he replied.

"Not Jule," she said. "You shouldn't use contractions. Your name is Julius."

Turning to the next boy, she asked: "What's your name?"

"Billious," he replied.

661. Three women went to a psychiatrist with their young daughters. The psychiatrist examined the first woman and said, "Madam, you have a deep subconscious urge for money and so you named your daughter Penny."

The second lady, a large woman, went in and the psychiatrist said, "Madam, you have a deep subconscious urge for sweets and so you named your little girl Candy."

The third woman, hearing this, took her little girl by the hand and said, "Come Schenley dear, we're leaving."

Nature

662. Nature is amazing; who would have thought of growing a fly swatter on the rear end of a cow?

Nuclear Age

663. When the lady who was making out the application came to the little square marked "Age," she did not hesitate. She simply wrote: "Nuclear."

664. A group of nuclear scientists held a convention at Las Vegas, and one of the professors spent all of his free time at the gambling tables. A couple of his colleagues were discussing their friend's weakness.

"Fenwick gambles as if there were no tomorrow," one said.
"Maybe," commented the other, "he knows something."

Nudism—Nudity

665. Life's greatest mystery—what nudists do with their keys after locking the car.

666. An engaged couple, nudists, decided to break up. The reason? "We've been seeing too much of each other."

667. "Why the apple for your trademark?" a client asked the tailor.
"Well, if it weren't for the apple, where would the clothing business be today?"

668. The two young nudists were being shown around the colony. One thing puzzled them . . . an old man wore an anklelength beard.
"Why do you wear that long beard?" they asked him.
"Somebody's got to go out for coffee," was the answer.

669. A midwest farmer got fed up with the cars which constantly sped past his property, endangering the lives of his children and his livestock. He finally solved the problem by erecting a sign that had cars literally creeping past his place. The sign said: "Slow Down for Nudist Camp Crossing."

670. An elderly Florida gent with a mild heart condition was ordered to lose some weight. A friend spotted him sitting on the beach off the Gulf of Mexico, avidly watching cavorting bathing beauties in their scant bikinis.
"Thought you were told to get some exercise?"
"That's right."
"Well, you'll never get it sitting here on the beach."
"That's where you're wrong," smiled the old gentleman. "I walk three miles every day just to watch them."

O

Occupation—Occupations

671. Two little girls were discussing their fathers. One, boasting, said, "My daddy is a dentist."

"That's nothing," retorted the other. "My daddy is a civil serpent."

672. Two disillusioned college presidents were discussing what they'd do if they had their lives to live over.

"I think I'd like to run an orphanage," said one. "No parents to contend with."

"I'd rather run a penitentiary," said the other. "No alumni pressure groups."

Office Humor

673. Sign in a professional office:

OFFICE HOURS

OPEN MOST DAYS ABOUT 9 OR 10
OCCASIONALLY AS EARLY AS 7, BUT SOME DAYS
AS LATE AS 12 OR 1
WE CLOSE ABOUT 5:30 OR 6
OCCASIONALLY ABOUT 4 OR 5, BUT
SOMETIMES AS LATE AS 11 OR 12
SOME DAYS OR AFTERNOONS, WE
AREN'T HERE AT ALL, AND LATELY
I'VE BEEN HERE JUST ABOUT ALL THE TIME,
EXCEPT WHEN I'M SOMEPLACE ELSE,
BUT I SHOULD BE HERE THEN, TOO.

Opinion

674. Two new products engineers were discussing their recent inventions. "What's your opinion of my newest idea?" asked the first.

"It is absolutely worthless," replied the second engineer.

"I know that," the first engineer responded, "but give it to me anyway."

Outer space

675. Your money goes further these days. In fact, a lot of it winds up in outer space.

676. Rumor has it that the latest guided missile is to be named "Civil Service Servant." You can't fire it, it won't work, and it's costing the taxpayer a fortune.

677. The latest in outer space people landing on earth concerns the sensitive little one who descended on New York recently. Walking by a store window, he looked in and saw a piano.

"Okay, you!" he snarled. "Wipe that nasty smile off your face!"

Overweight

678. You can depend on overweight people—they will never stoop to anything low.

679. The best way to lose weight is to eat all you want of everything you don't like.

680. The five-year-old was showing a kindergarten classmate the new weight scale in the bathroom.

"What's it for?" the visitor asked.

"I don't know," the five-year-old replied. "All I know is, when you stand on it, it makes you very mad."

681. "For years I've been weighing myself on one of those scales that hands out little cards. When I started I weighed 140 pounds. Now I weigh 180."

"How come you gained so much?"
"My pockets are full of little cards."

682.   An attractive young lady stepped on the drugstore scales after devouring a giant sundae and was shocked at what she saw. Promptly she slipped off her coat. The results were still unflattering, so she slid off her shoes. But then she discovered she was out of pennies. Without a moment's hesitation, the young man behind the soda fountain stepped forward.

"Don't stop now," he volunteered. "I've got a handful of pennies and they're all yours."

Parent—Child

683. There is only one beautiful child in the world and every parent has it.

684. The easiest way to teach children the value of money is to borrow some from them.

685. *Father:* "Eat your dinner!"
Child: "Motivate me!"

686. *Baby sitter (greeting the returning parents):* "Don't apologize. I wouldn't be in a hurry to come home either!"

687. Parents spend the first three years of a child's life trying to get him to talk. . .and the next sixteen trying to get him to shut up.

688. "I guess I'm wasting my advice on my son."
"No, you're not. Twenty years from now he'll be using the same advice on his son."

689. *Mother:* "I'm so glad to see you sitting so quietly while your father naps."
Junior: "I'm watching his cigarette burn down to his fingers."

690. "Mary," said her mother reprovingly, "every time you disobey, I get another gray hair."
"Gee, Mom," Mary answered, "so it was you who gave grandma all her gray hair."

691. The Scouts were in camp. In an inspection, the director found an umbrella neatly rolled inside the bedroll of a small Scout. As an umbrella was not listed as a necessary item, the director asked the boy to explain.

"Sir," answered the young man with a weary sigh, "did you ever have a mother?"

692. "How quickly can I learn French?" asked the young woman.

"That depends upon you," replied the teacher. "Why are you in such a rush?"

"We've just adopted a French baby only six months old," she answered, "and we want to be able to understand him when he starts to talk."

693. Like every other president, William Howard Taft had to endure his share of abuse. One night at the dinner table his youngest boy made a disrespectful remark to him. There was a sudden hush. Taft became thoughtful.

"Well," said Mrs. Taft, "aren't you going to punish him?"

"If the remark was addressed to me as his father he certainly will be punished," said Taft. "However, if he addressed it to the President of the United States, that is his Constitutional privilege."

Partnership

694. Two brothers in a farmer's elevator business had an intricate problem. One of them had taken an interest in the history and theory of ethics.

"It's a fine thing for you to study ethics," the first brother said, "but if I study ethics too, who's gonna weigh the corn?"

695. A twenty-year business partnership enjoyed by Sam and Pete ended very abruptly when Sam had to take a week off after catching a virus. On the third day of Sam's indisposition, Pete called from the office and said in an excited voice:

"There's $5,000 missing from the safe, Sam. What shall I do?"

"Put it back," Sam ordered coldly.

696. A story of modern-day entrepreneurs tells of the woman who, upon meeting a friend, told him she was going into business.

"What sort of business?" the friend asked.

"A partnership," the other replied.

"Are you putting in much capital?"

"No. I put in no capital. I put in the experience."

"And he puts in the capital, is that it?"

"Yes. We go into business for three years. He puts in the capital and I put in the experience. At the end of three years I will have the capital; and he will have the experience."

Percentage

697. The doctor explained to Higgins that he had a serious ailment for which an operation was abolutely imperative.

The patient turned pale and asked, "Isn't it very dangerous?"

"Yes," the doctor replied. "Five out of six who undergo this operation die, but as for you, you have nothing to worry about."

"Why not?" eagerly inquired the patient.

"Well, you see, you're a cinch to recover because my last five patients died," the doctor reassured him.

Perceptions

698. At the beginning of his circus career, master entertainer P. T. Barnum originated a museum display called "The Happy Family." Barnum's display featured a lion, tiger, panther, and baby lamb, all dwelling harmoniously in the same cage. His unique collection made newspaper headlines and people flocked to see this popular exhibit.

After the exhibit had been running for several weeks, a friend asked Barnum how everything was going.

"Oh, pretty well," Barnum replied. "The display will become a permanent feature if the supply of lambs holds out!"

699. "Tommy, please use the word 'fascinate' in a sentence," instructed the fifth grade teacher.

"Fascinate?" questioned Tommy.

"Yes. Just use the word in a simple sentence."

"My sister went to the shopping mall on Saturday," began Tommy, "to purchase a new blouse. The clerk showed a nice blouse with ten buttons on the front. When my sister tried the blouse on, it was too small and she was only able to fascinate (fasten eight) buttons."

Perfection

700.   A young American singer making his bow at La Scala was flattered when the discerning Italian audience forced him to return and sing an aria for the fourth time. Completely winded, he finally begged off, saying it was physically impossible to sing it a fifth time.

A voice boomed from the gallery: "You'll keep on singing it until you sing it right."

Point of view

701.   What is called "congestion" in the subway is called "intimacy" in a night club.

702.   *Mom (hearing a crash):* "More dishes, Junior?"
Junior: "No, Mom, fewer dishes."

703.   On the way to the hospital a nurse was hitting a pretty fast pace. She failed to heed the stoplight on the corner. John Law caught up with her in the next block. Said he: "Doesn't that red light remind you of something?"

Replied the nurse: "Oh, yes, someone wants the bed pan."

704.   Three people of different occupations looked at the Grand Canyon.

The archaeologist said: "What a wonder of science!"

The clergy said: "One of the glories of God!"

The cowboy said: "A heck of a place to lose a cow!"

705.   An outraged three-year-old howled his indignation when his mother told him she was locking the porch gate to keep him in. Sometime later, however, when the father locked the gate to the playroom, the youngster made no objection. Dad explained to his son that the gate was being locked to keep his mother from bothering him.

706. "Look here," said the angry hardware dealer to the sales clerk, "you told me that those mouse traps you sold me were wonderful for mice but my customers are complaining that they haven't caught a single mouse in them!"

"Well," was the salesperson's calm reply, "isn't that wonderful for the mice?"

707. An astronomer once remarked to Bishop Fulton J. Sheen:

"To an astronomer people are nothing but infinitesimal dots in an infinite universe."

"An interesting point of view," remarked the bishop, "but you seem to forget that your infinitesimal dot of a person is still the astronomer."

708. A young man who recently toured England was telling of his indignation over an incident that occurred when he visited the Tower of London. He said an affable Briton approached him with the remark, "American, aren't you? I thought so, from your accent."

"The nerve of the guy, making a crack like that," exclaimed the American, "when he was the one who had the accent!"

709. A monkey was negotiating for a consignment of coconuts with another monkey who had a reputation as a sharp trader. But they were far apart on price, and the prospective buyer was fuming around in the treetops wondering whether or not to increase his offer.

"Now look, Egmont," said his wife, finally. "You go down there and you stick to your original figure. If he haggles, tell him he's wasting his breath. Be firm, Egmont! Don't let him make a man of you."

710. A friend of mine, looking for an apartment to stay in during several months' visit to London, thought she'd found the real thing when she spotted an ad in the local paper. It read: "Lavishly furnished flat with excellent view overlooking shrubs and trees, also large variety of flowers and works of stone. Reasonable rent."

She phoned the number indicated, made an appointment, and went along to view the place. It seemed perfect. Then she glanced out of the window at the view. The flat overlooked a cemetery!

711. A salesperson delayed longer than usual by one of her customers could not make her regular overnight stop and had to put up in a small country inn. The next morning at breakfast the smiling innkeeper asked, "Did you enjoy the cornet concert in the next room last night?"

The sleepy salesperson shook her head angrily. "Enjoy it! I spent half the night pounding on the wall trying to get that idiot to stop his racket and go to bed."

"There certainly has been a misunderstanding," snapped the innkeeper, his smile gone. "My son told me he hated to disappoint you the way you kept pounding for more, but after he played every piece he knew five or six times, he simply had to stop and get some sleep."

712. An old story tells of two men who were walking along the streets of London, when the music of some wonderful chimes in a nearby cathedral floated through the air. One of the men remarked to the other, "Isn't that wonderful music?"

"I didn't hear what you said," replied the other.

"Aren't those chimes beautiful?" repeated the first speaker. But again the other man failed to catch the words, and the first speaker said for the third time, "Isn't that lovely music?"

"It's no use," came the answer. "Those pesky bells are making so much noise I can't hear what you say."

713. "Look at that one—the one staring at us through the bars. Doesn't he look intelligent?"

"Yes. There's something uncanny about it."

"He looks as if he understood every word we're saying."

"Walks on his hind legs, too, and swings his arms."

"There! He's got a peanut. Let's see what he does with it."

"Well, what do you know about that! He knows enough to take off the shell before he eats it, like we do."

"That's a female alongside of him. Listen to her chatter at him. He doesn't seem to be paying much attention to her though."

"She must be his mate."

"They look kind of sad, don't they?"

"Yes, I guess they wish they were in here with us monkeys."

714.   Did you read about the man driving down a residential street when a white poodle ran in front of his car and was killed.

The furious owner screamed at the man for not being more careful. "This is a disastrous loss to me!" the dog owner yelled. "I loved that dog like a child."

The driver was very apologetic at first. But no matter how he apologized, the woman wouldn't listen. Finally, frustrated, he said he could replace the dog.

Suddenly the woman calmed down, looked the man in the eyes, smiled wryly, and said: "You flatter yourself."

Police

715.   The police station had been quiet most of the week. Things were so slow the detectives were playing cards to pass the time. "What a life," grumbled one of the officers. "No fights, no thefts, no riots, no murders, no nothin'."

"Rest easy, Mike," said the captain. "Things'll break soon. You just gotta have faith in human nature."

Politeness

716.   The pompous and arrogant customer in the antique shop was obviously just passing the time, making the owner drag out fragile old pieces and then commenting on their poor quality and high prices. After about an hour of this, she looked at her watch and said she must go.

"I suppose," she said, "that you think I'm a nuisance, just trying to pretend that I know what I'm talking about."

The owner bowed graciously. "If you say so," he said. "In my shop, the customer is always right."

Politicians

717. Jay Leno says, "I saw a senator on a Sunday morning talk show who said that actions of the Senate have created jobs for a lot of citizens. Yeah, but let's face it—you can't make a career out of jury duty."

Quoted in The Wall Street Journal

718. A candidate for city council was speaking before a local service club. His hour-long rambling and pointless comments drew numerous yawns and frustrating sighs. Finally, the candidate closed his speech asking if there were any questions.

"I have one," a bored listener responded. "Who else is running?"

Politics

719. Two political candidates were having a hot debate. Finally, one of them jumped up and yelled at the other: "What about the powerful interest that controls you?"

And the other screamed back: "You leave my spouse out of this."

720. When the youthful Tom Dewey announced his candidacy for the presidency at the 1940 Republican convention, crusty old Harold Ickes, New Deal Secretary of the Interior, commented: "I see that Dewey has thrown his diaper into the ring."

721. At a victory celebration for his opponent the Senator who had been swept out of office by a political landslide, was called upon for a few remarks. He rose and dryly said: "I am reminded of an epitaph on an old tombstone in the town cemetery which read: 'I expected this, but not so soon.'"

722. A politician who had changed her views rather radically was congratulated by a colleague. "I'm glad you've seen the light," he said.

"I didn't see the light," came the terse reply. "I felt the heat."

723. We expect to find a doctor practicing medicine, a lawyer practicing law, an engineer engaged in engineering projects, school teachers teaching school; but when it comes to politics, we think there is something reprehensible in the fact that those engaged in politics are politicians.

724. A prominent member of Congress once was pleading his case before some hostile voters, a heavy stone was thrown at him, which, as he happened to stoop at that instant, passed over his head.

"You see," he said to friends who congratulated him on his narrow escape, "if I had been an upright politician, I would have been killed."

725. "Well," the little old lady finally admitted to the persistent politician, "you're my second choice."

"I'm honored, ma'am," he gushed. "But may I ask—who's your first?"

"Oh," she said casually, "anybody else who's running."

726. Like all political fights, the Jackson-Van Buren contest had its bitter moments. One young voter, at a political rally, cried out: "Three cheers for Jackson!" A Van Buren adherent promptly shouted angrily: "Three cheers for a jackass!"

"Okay," laughed the youth, "we won't quarrel. You cheer for your man and I'll cheer for mine."

727. A Vermonter had seventeen children, all boys. When they came of age, they voted uniformly for the Republican ticket—all except one boy. The father was asked to explain this terrible fall from grace.

"Well," he said, "I've always tried to bring them boys up right, in the fear of the Lord and Republicans to the bone, but John, the ornery cuss, got to readin'."

728. During a California senatorial contest many years ago, one of the candidates was being maligned badly. A voter wired him thus: "A report receiving wide circulation here that your children have not been baptized. Telegraph denial immediately."

The reply came back: "Sorry to say, report is correct. I have no children."

729.   A woman was arrested for speeding. The traffic officer asked to see her driver's license. It was a restricted license and it read she must always wear her glasses while driving. The officer seeing she was wearing none, said: "Where are your glasses?"

"But officer, I have Contacts," she replied.

"I don't care who your friends are. I am going to give you a ticket anyway," he said.

730.   While campaigning in a rural section of the Midwest for a congressional seat, a politician ran into an unfriendly crowd at one stop, and halfway through his speech was suddenly pelted with tomatoes and over-ripe fruit.

His presence of mind, however, did not fail him, and his next remark as he wiped the missiles off his face and shirt front turned boos into cheers. "My critics," he said jauntily, "may not think I know much about farm problems—but they'll have to admit I'm being a big help with the farm surplus!"

731.   Franklin Delano Roosevelt met an old neighbor during the third term campaign. "Whom are you voting for this year?" Roosevelt asked.

"The Republicans," the man said.

"How come?" Roosevelt asked. "Third term issue bothering you?"

"It's not that at all, Franklin," the neighbor said. "It's just that—well—I voted Republican the first time you ran, I voted Republican the second time you ran, and I'm going to vote Republican again because I never had it so good."

732.   A Texas oil tycoon offered to throw the biggest gold-arned victory party for Lyndon Johnson this country or any other country ever saw. "It'll be a two-hundred-and-fifty-thousand-dollar complimentary banquet in honor of Johnson's election to the office of President of the United States," he said.

"Fine," said a friend. "But supposin' he don't win the election."

The Texan replied. "Then we'll have the complimentary banquet in honor of his defeat."

733. Governor Robert Bradford of Massachusetts set down these attributes for a successful politician: "To live long in politics, you must possess the hide of a rhinoceros, the memory of an elephant, the persistence of a beaver, the native friendliness of a mongrel pup. You need the heart of a lion and the stomach of an ostrich. And it helps to have the humor and ubiquity of the crow. But all of these combined are not enough, unless when it comes to matters of principle, you also have the stubbornness of an army mule."

734. George E. Allen, once President Eisenhower's golf and bridge buddy, said that President Roosevelt liked best this joke on himself. A dyed-in-the-wool New Deal-hater in Westchester commuted to New York daily and criticized Roosevelt every inch of the way. Reaching Grand Central, he always rushed to the newsstand, bought a *Times*, glanced over the front page and handed it back to the newsdealer. Finally, the dealer asked him why he never looked at the inside of the paper.

"I'm only interested in finding a certain obituary," the enemy said.

"But the obituaries are on page 24," the dealer suggested.

"The so and so I'm looking for," said the man of firm habit, "will be on page one."

735. The margin of a single vote has been responsible for many of the great decisions, victories, defeats and disappointments of history.

Thomas Jefferson was elected President by one vote in the electoral college. So was John Quincy Adams. Rutherford B. Hayes was elected President by one vote. His election was contested; referred to an electoral commission, the matter was again decided by a single vote. The man who had cast the deciding vote for President Hayes was himself elected to Congress by a margin of one vote. That one vote was cast by a voter who, though desperately ill, insisted on being taken to the polls.

Marcus Morton was elected governor of Massachusetts by one vote. Countless mayors, legislators, councilpeople, and other public officials have enjoyed the sweet wine of victory or the bitter gall of defeat by a single vote. California, Washington, Idaho, Texas and Oregon gained statehood by one vote.

The ill-considered War of 1812 was brought about by a series of events based upon a single vote.

Power

736. Three lobbyists in Washington, D.C. were debating how to measure their degree of power with the White House.

"I would know I was influential," began one, "if the President would invite me over for a private dinner."

"That would be impressive," responded the second. "However, I would know I had influence if the President would invite me to dinner and while we were dining, his hotline rang and he didn't answer it. That would be the ultimate."

"Let me tell you the real measure of power," responded the third lobbyist. "I would know I was powerful if the President invited me to dinner. Then, while talking over coffee, his hotline rang. The President answers and listens momentarily and then looking at me, he says, 'Here, it's for you.' Now that's power!"

Preaching

737. The average person's idea of a good sermon is one that goes over their head—and hits one of their neighbors.

738. The sermon went on and on. Finally, the priest paused and asked, "What more, my friends, can I say?"

From the rear of the nave came a hollow voice: "Amen."

739. During Sunday services the minister told his congregation:

"Today I've prepared a fifty dollar sermon, a twenty dollar sermon and a ten dollar sermon."

After a brief pause, he continued: "We will now take up the collection and see which one it will be."

Precaution

740. There's a manufacturer who lost a fortune in the stock market and now won't even read a book with margins in it.

741. "My good man," said the dentist. "You don't have to pay me now."

"Pay you?" said the patient. "I'm counting my money before you gimme the gas."

742.   Many years Iowa's football coach had a devoutly religious housekeeper. After a Rose Bowl victory, Hawkeye fans presented the coach with a new car. He drove it home, pulled up in front of his house, and strolled to the front porch.

"What do you think?" the coach asked the housekeeper.

The good woman appraised him silently, then said, "Just remember the same people who praised Jesus also crucified Him."

Predictions

743.   In Mark Twain's masterpiece, *136 Varieties of New England Weather,* he referred to forecasters as being unpredictable so their predictions sound like this: "Probably northeast to southwest winds, varying to the southward and westward and eastward and points in between; high and low barometer sweeping around from place to place; probable areas of rain, snow, hail, and drought succeeded or preceded by earthquakes, with thunder and lightning."

Premium—Premiums

744.   A bride was showing a friend the kitchen of her new, seven-room house.

"We furnished the kitchen with soap coupons," the bride said.

"With soap coupons!" the friend exclaimed. "What about the other six rooms?"

"Oh, those," the bride replied, "they're filled with soap."

Preoccupation

745.   *Doctor:* "You've simply got to have more diversion and relaxation."

Patient: "But, doctor, I'm too busy."

Doctor: "Nonsense! The ants are hard-working creatures, but they always take time to attend all the picnics."

746. An Omaha woman, caught short on groceries for her husband's breakfast and lunch, rushed to the store for food. With her she took five-year-old Terry.

"Hey, mom, can I tell you something?" puffed Terry as they rushed to the store.

"No, Terry, I'm too busy," said his mother.

At the store, Terry tried again, "Hey, mom. . ."

"Don't bother me. I'm trying to think," his mother interrupted.

Finally at home, Terry said, "Now can I tell you?"

"Oh, yes, what is it?" said his mother in exasperation.

"I wanted to tell you that the zipper on your shorts is unzipped."

Presidential Humor

747. Crowd estimates are always a bone of contention between the press and presidential candidates. Benjamin Bradlee, in his book, *Conversations with Kennedy*, tells about a rally that JFK advisors said was attended by 35,000 people. Traveling reporters thought this figure to be extremely high. Bradlee asked Kennedy how they arrived at this figure and with his quick wit, Kennedy responded: "Plucky (Press Secretary Pierre Salinger's nickname) counts the nuns and then multiplies by 100."

748. Abraham Lincoln was a master with humor. One day he was challenged to a duel by a southern gentleman. Lincoln agreed to the confrontation under the condition he could choose the weapon and the location. After the gentleman agreed to those conditions, Lincoln responded, "Cow dung at five feet."

749. According to Hendrick Hertzberg in *The New Republic*, Bob Hope threw a pre-election party at his home for George Bush. The host admitted to being disturbed by the actions of the Secret Service. "They brought in dogs to sniff around for bombs," Hope said. "They stopped twice at my joke files."

750. The 1987 Soviet-American Summit resulted in historic changes in the Intermediate-Range Nuclear Forces Treaty. Although serious in nature, the summit was laced with tasteful humor. Columnist Hugh Sidey provided an excellent summary in the December 28, 1987 issue of *Time:* When historians write of this summitry between once glowering superpowers, they may decide that the sense of humor shared by the two leaders played as much a part as any other human quality. "He has a good sense of humor," Reagan declared. "I told him the speeding joke. The Soviet police were told to give tickets to speeders, no matter who they were. One day Gorbachev is late leaving home for the Kremlin, and he hurries to his car and tells the driver that he will drive to save time. So the driver sits in the back seat and Gorbachev takes off lickety-split down the road and passes two cops on the side. One of the officers gives chase but in a short time returns to his partner, who asks if he gave him a ticket. 'No,' the cop answers. 'Well, who in the world was it?' asks the other cop. 'I don't know,' replied the first cop, 'but his driver was Gorbachev.' Gorbachev loved it. He just howled."[1]

751.   The preacher was vexed because a certain member of his congregation always went to sleep during the sermon. As the man was snoring in the front row one Sunday, the preacher determined he would fix him once and for all.

In a whisper, he asked the congregation, "All who want to go to heaven, please rise." Awaking with a start, the sleepyhead jumped to his feet and saw the preacher standing tall and angry in the pulpit. "Well, sir," he said, "I don't know what we're voting on, but it looks like you and me are the only ones for it."

Quoted by Lyndon B. Johnson in All the President's Wits
(Morrow), by Gerald Gardner

752.   President Coolidge invited a group of people to cruise the Potomac on the Presidential yacht. As he stood alone at the rail, looking out at the expanse of water, someone exclaimed, "Look at that slight and slender figure! Look at that head, bowed over the rail! What thoughts are in the mind of this man, burdened by the problems of the nation?"

Finally, Coolidge turned around, and joined the others, saying, "See that sea gull over there? Been watching it for twenty minutes. Hasn't moved. I think he's dead!"

---

[1] Hugh Sidey, "The Presidency," *Time,* December 28, 1987, p. 22, 1987, Time Inc.

753. Abraham Lincoln was comfortable laughing at and making fun of his personal appearance. On one occasion, he reflected: "Sometimes I feel like the ugly man who met an old woman traveling through a forest. The old woman said, 'You're the ugliest man I ever saw.' "

"I can't help it," the ugly man said.

" 'No, I guess not,' " the woman admitted, " 'but the least you could do is stay at home.' "

Prevention

754. An English journalist asked the sergeant of police in a Fermanagh village about the size of the police force.

"I have three," said the sergeant.

"With yourself, that's four. Surely there isn't enough work in this small place to keep four of you going?" the reporter asked.

"Well," said the sergeant, "there is not, but if we weren't here there would be."

Problems

755. Whenever I feel overwhelmed by one of life's little problems, I reflect on the story Pope John XXIII told about himself. He confessed, "It often happens that I wake at night and begin to think about a serious problem and decide I must tell the Pope about it. Then I wake up completely and remember I am the Pope."

756. Two business retailers were discussing the difficulties of their trade. "I can't remember business ever being this bad," Joe commented. "My April sales were the worst I've seen in several years. Then June came along. What a disaster. And July was even worse."

"You haven't seen anything," groaned his friend. "My son dropped out of college and joined a commune. My teenage daughter told me yesterday she was pregnant and plans to drop out of high school. And now my marriage partner for the last 23 years tells me there is no love left in our relationship. It doesn't get any worse than this."

"Oh yes it does," replied Joe. "My August sales."

Procrastination

757. Never finish anything you haven't started.

758. The story is told of a company president who had little tolerance for procrastination. In an effort to increase organizational efficiency, she hung up signs throughout the building that said, "DO IT NOW." Within twenty-four hours, her vice-president quit, her secretary got married, and the custodian stole the company delivery van.

Profanity

759. *Mother:* "What did your father say when he fell off the ladder?"
Junior: "Shall I leave out the naughty words?"
Mother: "Of course, dear."
Junior: "Nothing."

760. "Boss," said the dock supervisor, "the dockworkers are a little leary of the new freight loader you hired yesterday."
"Why so?" asked the terminal manager. "He checked out well."
"Maybe so," replied the dock supervisor, "but this morning he stubbed his toe on a crate of iron castings and said, 'Oh, the perversity of inanimate objects.' "

Professional fees

761. A patient once complained to his psychiatrist that he was always forgetting things. "What shall I do?" he asked.
"Pay me in advance," the doctor advised.

762. *Lawyer:* "When I was a boy, my highest ambition was to be a pirate."
Client: "Congratulations!"

763. Upon receiving the bill for the extraction of a tooth, Pete phoned his dentist and complained. "Why that's three times what you usually charge!"
"Yes, I know," replied the dentist, "but you yelled so loud you scared away two other patients!"

764. A physician presented her bill to the courts as a legal way of collecting fees due from a deceased person's estate. "Do you wish my bill sworn to?" the doctor asked.

"No," said the legalite. "Death of the deceased is sufficient evidence that you attended him professionally."

765. "Whenever I have a headache," explained the patient to his doctor, "I take aspirin. When I have a cold, I go to bed and drink fruit juices. If I have stomach trouble, I take bicarbonate of soda. Have I been doing the right things?"

"Yes, you have," replied the doctor. "That will be thirty dollars, please."

766. Nobody has made much fuss about it, but the doctors in Beverly Hills, California, are pretty expensive these days. Recently a man fell down a flight of stairs and hurt his leg. He went to the doctor who fixed him up. As he was leaving, the doctor said to him, "Don't worry! You'll be walking before the day is over." He was right. The doctor took the man's car for his fee.

767. There was a young nursing student who broke her engagement to a doctor, and she was telling her girl friend about it.

"Do you mean to say," exclaimed her friend, wide-eyed, "he actually asked you to give back all his presents?"

"Not only that," sniffed the young student, "he sent me a bill for 36 visits!"

768. The prisoner had sent for the town's leading lawyer.

"Have you anything by way of cash for my fee?" the attorney wanted to know.

"No, but I've got a new Ford car."

"Well, that's fine. That will do. And what is the charge they are holding against you?"

The prisoner replied, "Stealing a new Ford car."

769. After giving the new patient a thorough diagnostic examination and prescribing medicines and special foods, the Park Avenue doctor announced that his fee would be $100.

The visitor blanched, "That's almost as much as I make in a week."

The doctor offered to reduce the bill to $75. Still the man protested. After much haggling, the MD reluctantly accepted $10. "But why," he asked, "did you come to a specialist like me? Why not a charity clinic? That wouldn't cost you anything."

"Oh, no. When I'm sick, money's no object."

Professions

770. If lawyers are disbarred and clergy deflocked, doesn't it follow that electricians can be delighted; musicians denoted; cowboys deranged; tree surgeons debarked; and dry cleaners depressed?

Virginia Ostman

771. A newly hired postal service employee was being trained by a less-than-motivated veteran. Each day they would complete the delivery route in the familiar postal jeep. One morning the veteran jumped out of the jeep, walked 20 feet behind the vehicle, and began beating a turtle to death. The new employee was astounded. "What did you do that for?" he asked.

"That blasted turtle has been our tail for three days," responded the veteran.

772. A passenger in a small commuter plane was startled when the pilot began to laugh uncontrollably. "What's so funny?" asked the passenger. Getting control of himself, the pilot responded: "Oh, I was just thinking what they will say at the prison when they find out I have escaped."

773. Bob Orben writing in *Current Comedy* has a good point: "If space scientists are so smart, why do they all count backwards?"

774. Sign in financial consultant's office:

QUESTIONS ANSWERED

Simple	$0.50
Guesses	$1.00
Intelligent	$2.50
Honest	$5.00

DUMB LOOKS ARE STILL FREE

775. A doctor, an engineer, and a consultant stood outside the pearly gates, awaiting their admittance. St. Peter suddenly appeared and announced he could only admit one—the person with the oldest profession.

"That's me," the doctor said confidently. "As soon as God created Adam, he performed an operation. He took a rib from Adam's side and created Eve. Surgery is the oldest profession."

"Wait a moment," replied the engineer. "Before God created Adam and Eve, he overcame the chaos and confusion that existed and constructed the earth in six days. Engineering came before surgery."

"You're both wrong," said the consultant. "Who do you think created the chaos and confusion?"

Professionalism

776. Did you hear about the young man who couldn't get his quarter to work in a pay telephone? It was solid silver and the edges as well as the markings had worn smooth. After several attempts and an equal number of rejections, the young man placed the quarter in an envelope and mailed it to the U. S. Mint. Along with the quarter, he forwarded a note requesting a replacement for his defective coin.

A few days later, he received his old quarter, along with an official note explaining the mint's inability to replace his quarter.

Several letters later the determined young man received another note explaining the depreciation of the quarter along with one dime, two nickels, and four pennies.

He learned what every football coach knows: "It's tough to get a 'good quarter back.' "

Promise—Promises

777. Three turtles decided they would go on a picnic down on the banks of the Willamette River. They packed their lunches and arrived at the river. Before they could begin eating, it started to rain. They decided one must go back after an umbrella so that they could eat in the dry. The smallest turtle was the one who finally agreed to go if the others would promise not to eat the sandwiches while he was gone. It was agreed.

They waited a day, a week, a month, until finally a year had gone by. Still the turtle did not return. . . . Finally, one turtle said to the other, "He's not coming back, let's go ahead and eat the sandwiches." Just then the little turtle stuck his head from behind the nearby rock and said, "If you do, I won't go."

Proof

778. The trouble with being best man at a wedding is that you get no chance to prove it.

779. "And you still insist you're innocent," repeated the judge, "in spite of the proof that seven witnesses saw you steal the necklace?"

"If it's witnesses you want, sir," replied the defendant, "I can produce seventy who didn't see me steal it."

780. Two men who loved to argue stood on a street curb in Warsaw watching a regiment of infantry march past. For no apparent reason one of them turned to the other and said, "You claim to be a scholar. Can you tell me, do people grow upward or downward?"

"Downward, of course," replied the other.

"How do you know that?" asked the first.

"Very simple," replied the second man. "When I outgrow my overcoat it becomes too short for me at the bottom."

"Ah, but look at those soldiers marching by," said the first one. "Do they not prove that people grow upward?"

"In what way, pray?" asked the second one.

"Because, as you can readily see, they are all even at the bottom and uneven at the top."

Psychiatrist—Psychiatrists

781. A young psychiatrist, haggard with the troubles of his patients, got into the elevator of a New York hospital with an elderly but sprightly senior consultant.

"How on earth do you remain so youthful, sir?" sighed the younger man, "listening year after year to all those terrible complaints, anxieties and fears?"

The older man shrugged his shoulders: "Who listens?"

Psychiatry

782. *Psychiatrist to patient:* "Despite what you think, Mr. Jones, you don't have a complex. Actually, you *are* inferior."

783. *Psychiatrist to patient:* "Did this feeling of being an insignificant pipsqueak come on suddenly, or did it develop normally with marriage and parenthood?"

784. A psychiatrist recently reported that half her patients went to her because they weren't married, while the other half went to her because they were.

785. A patient was informed by his psychiatrist that he could consider himself cured of his delusion that he was Napoleon.

"Oh, wonderful!"cried the happy man. "Where's the phone? I must call Josephine and tell her the great news."

786. "I see you were last employed by a psychiatrist," said the employer to the applicant. "Why did you leave?"

"Well," she replied, "I just couldn't win. If I was late to work, I was hostile. If I was early, I had an anxiety complex. If I was on time, I was compulsive."

787. A haggard man walked into a psychiatrist's office, tore open a cigarette and stuffed the tobacco up his nose.

"I see you really need me," the startled doctor remarked as he ran toward the man.

"Sure do," said the guy, "have you got a light?"

788. *Psychiatrist to patient:* "That'll be $100."

Patient: "Why $100? All the others only charge $50."

Psychiatrist: "It's part of the treatment. It will help you to attach less importance to money and material things."

789. A man insisted to his psychiatrist that he had swallowed a horse. None of the doctor's persuasive tactics could persuade him to change his mind. In desperation, the psychiatrist agreed to "operate." The idea was simply to put the patient under and bring a horse into the operating room.

When the patient came to, the doctor pointed to the horse and said: "Well, that won't worry you any more."

"That's not the one I swallowed," he said. "That's a bay. My horse was white."

790. After the psychiatrist had examined the child, she turned to the child's mother and said:

"I will see Johnny in a month again. But you also need help. You are far too upset and worried about your child. I suggest that you take these tranquilizers regularly until I see you again."

A month later, the mother brought her child to the psychiatrist.

"How is Johnny?" asked the doctor.

To which the mother replied: "Who cares?"

Public speaking

791. If a thing goes without saying, let it.

792. The person who rises to the occasion should know when to sit down.

793. *Speaker:* "I have only ten minutes and hardly know where to begin."

A voice: "Begin at the ninth."

794. A physician reports the sense of hearing is considerably dulled by eating. Which is nature's way of protecting us against after-dinner speakers.

795. Once upon a time a lion ate a bull and he felt so good that he roared and roared. A hunter heard him and killed him with one shot.

Moral: When you are full of bull, keep your mouth shut.

796. When Thomas Buckley first ran for auditor of Massachusetts in 1941, his speech consisted of but seven words: "I am an auditor," he said, "not an orator." He continued to run and win for years thereafter—with the same seven words!

797. A senator, who shall remain nameless, was approached in the corridor by a colleague, who asked: "How was your speech at the Democratic dinner last night?"

"Well," replied the first senator, with a puzzled look, "when I sat down, the toastmaster said it was the best thing I ever did. Now I'm wondering what he meant."

798.   The candidate's wife dropped heavily into an easy chair, kicked off her shoes and sighed: "Boy, what a day—I've never been so tired in my life."

"Why should you be tired?" growled her husband. "Think of me making seven speeches to the voters. You didn't have to do that."

"That's right," agreed the weary wife, "but, remember, I had to listen to 'em."

799.   Joseph H. Choate, one-time ambassador of Great Britain, was called upon at a dinner of the Pilgrim Fathers to respond to the toast, "The Pilgrim Fathers."

After paying tribute to the Pilgrim Fathers for enduring the rigors of the New England winters and the privations and dangers of life in the little settlement of Plymouth, he paused.

"But let us give thought," he added with a grin, "to the Pilgrim Mothers. For they not only had to endure everything the Pilgrim Fathers endured, but mark this, they had to endure, also, the Pilgrim Fathers."

800.   Once when J. Sterling Morton was making a speech, a man in the crowd shouted, "Louder!" Mr. Morton raised a voice which was always more sonorous than a whisper, but the man yelled "Louder!" again.

Mr. Morton once more put on steam, and his voice stretched out to the edges of the crowd as he lambasted the free silver apostasy of his well-known political enemy, William Jennings Bryan.

When the man for the third time yelled "Louder!" Mr. Morton paused for a moment and then continued:

"My friends, the time will finally come when the vast machinery of this universe must stop, and all the wheels, gears, and belts be motionless, when the spheres shall cease to roll, and the defined periods of time be lost in eternity.

"In that awful hour, my friends, the angel Gabriel will descend from the battlements of heaven, and place one foot on the land and the other on the sea. He will force a blast from his trumpet which will reverberate throughout the remotest corners of the universe. And when he does, some small-bore person will holler 'Louder! Louder'!"

Punctuality

801.   It's easy to tell those who have never had much experience in committee work—they always get to the meeting on time.

802.   "Norah," said the minister to the housekeeper. "I've asked Mr. and Mrs. James to dinner at 6:30, but I think I'll give them a quarter of an hour's grace."

"Well," replied the housekeeper, "I'm religious myself, but I think you're overdoing it."

803.   In most Federal offices, contrary to general belief, they place high value on punctuality. The story is told of an employee who showed up an hour late at the General Accounting Office. The worker limped, was bruised and battered about the face, and carried his arm in a sling. His section chief glowered at him and glanced meaningly at the clock.

"I fell out of the window," the timid worker explained.

"And that took you an hour?" his boss roared.

Punishment

804.   One of those amateur sopranos who seems to feel the urge to screech away at every opportunity was rendering some numbers in prison before a convict group.

The warden's young son was visiting him that evening and the boy took all this in with some awe. The warden winced a little as she reached for some high notes and he turned to his son and said: "Let this be a lesson to you should you ever feel tempted to do something wrong."

805.   Five-year-old Billy ran into the house to tell his mother that four-year-old Johnny had fallen into the fish pond. She ran out to the pond and found Johnny submerged up to his neck and yelling for help. After rescuing him, she asked Billy how it had happened.

"I kept telling him that he was going to fall into the pond if he got too close to the edge."

"But what made him fall in?" demanded his mother.

"I pushed him," was the matter-of-fact reply.

"What?" cried the mother.

"Yes, I pushed him," Billy repeated. "I wanted to show him what would happen if he didn't mind."

Purpose

806.   The neighborhood kids had congregated in the front yard when a fire truck zoomed past. Sitting on the front seat was a Boxer dog. The children fell to discussing the dog's duties in connection with the fire truck.

"They use him to keep the crowds back when they go to a fire," said a five-year-old girl.

"No," said another, "they carry him for good luck."

The third, a boy about six, brought the argument to an abrupt end. "They use the dog," he said firmly, "to find the fire plug."

Q

Qualification—Qualifications

807. There's at least one ineligible football star at every college. Same old story—he could run and kick, but he couldn't pass.

808. As the X-ray specialist walked down the aisle to say the marriage vows with a former patient, someone whispered: "I wonder what she saw in him?"

809. Lincoln called in Ben Wade and Senator Daniel Voorhees to discuss the appointment of an Indian commissioner, explaining what kind of man he wanted to appoint.

"My valuable advisors, for an Indian commissioner," said the President, "I want a pure-minded, moral, Christian person—frugal and self-sacrificing."

"I think," interrupted Voorhees, "that you won't find such a person."

"Why not?"

"Because, Mr. President, he was crucified about eighteen hundred years ago," said the senator.

Question—Answer

810. *Small boy:* "Daddy, why does it rain?"
Daddy: "It rains to make the lawn and flowers grow."
Small boy: "Then why does it rain on sidewalks?"

811. The head of a branch of the American Society for the Prevention of Cruelty to Animals had just hired a new typist, and he spent an hour explaining the work of the organization and the office routine.

"If you have any questions as you go along, don't be afraid to ask," he told her before returning to his desk.

A few minutes later the typist appeared in front of him. "I have a question," she said. "Is it all right if I swat a fly?"

812. A pastor of the parish always asked the children the same questions, and in the same sequence: "What is your name? How old are you? Did you say your prayers? What will happen to you if you don't say your prayers?"

An overly ambitious mother rehearsed her little boy with the answers, and when the pastor called, the boy beat him to the punch by rattling off: "Jerry Jones—5—yes—go to hell."

813. The lion was stalking through the jungle looking for trouble. He grabbed a passing tiger and asked, "Who is the king of the jungle?"

"You are, O mighty lion," answered the tiger.

The lion then grabbed a bear and asked, "Who is boss of the jungle?"

"You, O mighty lion," answered the bear.

Next the lion met an elephant and asked, "Who is boss of the jungle?" The elephant grabbed him with his trunk, whirled him around and threw him up against a tree, leaving him bleeding and broken. The lion got up feebly and said, "Just because you don't know the answer is no reason for you to get so rough."

814. A grandfather was alone at home for a few days while his wife visited one of their daughters. To his consternation another daughter came over and left one of his young grandsons to spend the night with him. The next morning grandpa got up and prepared a big bowl of oatmeal, his own favorite breakfast.

"Do you like sugar?" he asked the small boy.

The grandson nodded.

"How about some butter, too?"

Again the boy nodded.

"Of course, you like milk?"

"Sure," the boy replied.

When grandpa placed the steaming bowl of oatmeal with butter, sugar, and milk before him, the boy refused to eat it.

The grandfather was exasperated. "But when I asked you, didn't you say you liked sugar, butter, and milk?"

"Yes," replied the youngster, "but you didn't ask me if I liked oatmeal."

815. An old-timer strutted into a saloon and, in a heavy drawl, ordered a mint-julep. The bartender hesitated, but only for a moment before going to work on a concoction which he topped off with a green leaf. Smiling proudly he set the drink in front of his distinguished customer.

The man frowned as he sniffed the drink. He tilted the glass to sample its content, and then slammed the glass down. He stared angrily at the man behind the bar. "Sir," he said, in a much too affected drawl, "is this really a mint julep?"

The bartender looked pained, but only for a moment. "Are you really a genuine Southerner?" he asked politely.

"Indeed I am, sir," the man hastened to reply.

"Then," snapped the barkeeper, "you shouldn't have had to ask."

R

Real estate

816. Then there's the sad tale about the two-story house. The real estate salesperson told him one story before he bought it and another one afterward.

817. "There are advantages and disadvantages about this property," said the honest real estate agent.

"To the north is the gas works, to the east a glue factory, to the south a fish and chip shop, and to the west a sewage farm. Those are the disadvantages."

"What are the advantages?" asked the prospective buyer.

"You can alway tell which way the wind is blowing," said the agent.

Reciprocation

818. In the ladies lounge of a big city hotel there's a pay turnstile between the lounge and the lavatory. Four matrons were searching for change when one of them said: "No, Myrtle, you took us to lunch. This is my treat."

819. Mrs. Jackson and her husband were playing golf. Mr. Jackson's first tee shot sliced across the fairway and hit the husband of another woman out golfing.

The second wife stormed over to Mrs. Jackson. "Do you know what you did?" she shouted. "You hit my husband with your ball!"

"Sorry," said Mrs. Jackson, handing her a ball. "Have a shot at mine."

820. A very poor Chinese operated a small laundry next door to a more prosperous Chinese restaurant. Every day he would take his simple bowl of rice, place his chair as near as he dared to the restaurant, and sniff the appetizing aromas as he ate.

One day, he received a bill from his neighbor "for smell of food." He went into his laundry and came out with his tiny money box. This he rattled in the ears of his creditor, saying, "I hereby pay for the smell of your food with the sound of my money."

Religion

821. Two little boys were arguing about religion. "My priest knows more than your silly minister will ever hope to know." The other little boy quickly responded: "Well, he should, you tell him everything."

822. The pastor had some extensive repairs done on his automobile by a member of the congregation. The service manager indicated that the $500 for repairs was quite modest considering all the work that was completed. "Can you tell me why a $500 repair bill is modest," the minister began, "but a $50 donation to the church is substantial?"

823. A little boy returning home from his first circus, comments: "Once you've been to a circus, you'll never enjoy church again."

Religious Transformation

824. A young man entered the convention hall where a religious gathering was being held. He spotted one empty aisle seat near the front. "Is this chair saved?" he asked the man sitting next to the empty chair.

"I'm not sure," he responded, "but sit down and we'll pray for it together."

Resourcefulness

825. A practical medical school in Switzerland gives each graduating student a batch of ten-year-old copies of Newsweek magazine—so patients won't think they are new in the business.

826. "Didn't I hear the clock strike two as you came in last night?" asked the mother at the breakfast table.

"Yes, mother," the daughter replied sweetly from behind the morning paper. "It started to strike ten but I stopped it to keep from waking you."

827. As a woman approached her car in a crowded parking lot, a police officer stopped her. "Your license plates are on upside down!" he exlaimed. "I know," she explained brightly. "It saves me a lot of time. Now I don't have to wander over the whole lot looking for my car."

828. The wife of a prominent Englishman constantly declared that upon his death she would dance on his grave; and she repeated the jibe regularly throughout recurring attacks the poor man suffered, including his last. But in expiration he foiled her plan, for contained in his will was an irrevocable legal codicil directing that he be buried at sea.

829. A motorist overtook a young man running along the road. He stopped his car and asked the perspiring runner to get in.

"An emergency, I gather?" the driver asked.

"No," puffed the young man. "I always run like that when I want a ride. It seldom fails."

830. A young mother was worried about her nine-year-old son. No matter how much she scolded, he kept running around with his shirt tails flapping. On the other hand, her neighbor had four boys, and each of them always wore his shirt neatly tucked in. Finally, in desperation the young mother asked her neighbor to tell her the secret.

"Oh, it's all very simple," she replied. "I just take all their shirts and sew an edging of lace on the bottom."

831. Timmy had only a quarter in his pocket when he approached the farmer and pointed to a tomato hanging lusciously from a vine.

"Give you a quarter for it," the boy offered.

"That kind brings fifty cents," the farmer told him.

"This one?" Timmy asked, pointing to a smaller, greener and less tempting specimen. The farmer nodded agreement. "Okay," said Timmy, and sealed the deal by placing his two pennies in the farmer's hand. "I'll pick it up in about a week."

832. A famed explorer was captured by savages in the wilds of South America. They were dancing around him in preparation for the kill when an idea struck the explorer—he would awe them with "magic." From his pocket he took a cigarette lighter.

"See," he said, "I am a fire-maker!" And with a flick of his thumb, the lighter burst into flame. The savages fell back in astonishment.

"Magic!" cried the explorer in triumph.

"Sure is," replied the chief. "Only time we ever saw a lighter work the first time."

833. Here's a suggestion for parents who become naturally worried when their youngsters who are away from home, either at camp or college, neglect to write:

Just send the child your usual letter and then add a postscript something like this: "Hope you can use the $10 I am enclosing." Then don't enclose it.

The child may not have written home for a long time, but that appended message will bring a letter in a hurry. And your child will be sure to add their own little worried postscript, "I didn't find the $10 you mentioned."

834. A small truck loaded with glassware backed out of a factory driveway into the path of a large truck. Most of the glass was broken in the crash, and the driver seemed on the verge of tears. A big crowd gathered, and one benevolent old gentleman said compassionately:

"I suppose you will have to make this good out of your own pocket?"

"I'm afraid so," lamented the driver.

"Well, well," said the gentleman. "Here's a dollar for you. Let me pass your hat and I dare say some of these kind people will help you out, too."

Over a hundred people dropped bills into the outstretched hat. The driver, stowing the money away as the crowd dispersed, nodded toward the retreating back of the benevolent old gentleman.

"That's what I call a smart guy—he's my boss."

835. A rabbi and two friends, one a Protestant minister, and the other a Catholic priest, played three-handed cards for small stakes one night a week. Nothing wrong with that except they lived in a small town which did not allow such activity. The sheriff raided their game and brought all three before a justice of the peace, who after listening to the sheriff's story, sternly asked the priest:

"Were you gambling, Father?"

The priest looked heavenward, whispered, "Oh Lord, forgive me," then said aloud to the JP:

"No, your Honor, I was not gambling."

"Were you gambling, Reverend?" the JP asked the Protestant minister, who, like the priest, also looked upward and whispered for forgiveness before he answered the JP:

"No, your Honor, I was not gambling."

The JP addressed the third clergy person:

"Were you gambling, Rabbi?"

Looking the JP squarely in the eye, the rabbi shrugged and replied:

"With whom?"

Restaurant—Restaurants

836. *Waiter:* "We have practically everything on the menu."

Patron: "So I see. Can you bring me a clean one?"

837. The man sawed on his steak, and he jabbed it, but still he couldn't cut it. He called the waiter.

The waiter examined the steak. "Sorry, I can't take it back," he said. "You've already bent it."

838. The proprietor called her servers together and said:"I want you to look your best today. Give these doctors a big smile. Kid them a little, serve them quickly and get out of the way."

"What's the matter?" asked one server. "They having a special program?"

"Nope," replied the owner. "The beef's tough again."

839.   The clock in a restaurant window had stopped a few minutes past noon. One day a friend asked the owner if he knew the clock was not running. "Yes," replied the owner, "but you would be surprised to know how many people look at that clock, think they are hungry, and come in to get something to eat."

840.   The customer in the cafe had been waiting unattended for twenty minutes and finally, his patience exhausted, he called after a passing waitress: "Hi, Miss—can I see your manager—I have a complaint."

"Complaint," she said haughtily, eyeing him up and down. "This is a cafe, not a nursing home."

841.   She was one of those fussy customers who sometimes come into a restaurant. "Now mind you," she said, "I want my egg fried exactly 1 ½ minutes. The white part should be done real nice but I don't want the yolk to get too hard. About half a pinch of salt . . . no more, no less. A sniff of pepper. Oh, yes, make sure the frying pan isn't too greasy. And I like my eggs straight from the country."

"One thing, lady," said the waitress ever so sweetly. "The hen's name is Doris. Is that all right?"

Retirement

842.   *Retiree:* "Age is a matter of attitude. I'm retreaded, not retired."

843.   A letter of resignation from a woman who had quit to have a baby, said: "Dear Boss: I am getting too big for this job . . ."

Reunion, Class

844.   After returning from his 50th college reunion at a large midwestern university, the father told his son that it had been different from other reunions. "Why?" he asked.

"Well," he answered, "at the 50th reunion they put the men and women up in the same dormitories."

845. All day long Mrs. Smith's maid had gone around red-eyed and moping. Finally Mrs. Smith could stand it no longer. "For heaven's sake, Mary," she exclaimed, "what is the matter?"

"I—don't know how to tell you, ma'am," sobbed the maid, "but I overheard Mr. Smith talking on the telephone. And . . . Oh, ma'am. He said it in so many words. He's packing up and going back to his old girl friend this weekend."

"His old girl friend?" Mrs. Smith, though excited and suddenly suspicious, kept control. "He didn't happen to mention her name, did he, Mary?"

"That he did," said Mary, proudly. "And I got it, all right, Alma Mater."

Romance

846. A woman might as well propose; her husband will claim she did.

847. Is it better to have loved and lost or to have won and be bossed?

848. Lots of people can be had for a song. Trouble is, it's the wedding march.

849. "Four long years of college," sighed the college graduate, "and who has it got me?"

850. Single people can be compared to a baseball player—always trying to turn a single into a double.

851. He didn't want to marry her for her money, but he just couldn't figure out any other way to get it.

852. *Advice to singles:* Don't go looking for the ideal person, a spouse is much easier to find.

853. *Girl friend to boy friend at marriage-license bureau:* "Seems sort of silly to get a license after the hunting is over."

854. "Just give me my golf, the great outdoors, and a beautiful woman. . . and you can keep my golf and the great outdoors."

855. The only difference in the game of love over the last few thousand years is that they've changed trumps from clubs to diamonds.

856. The trouble with many people these days is that too often they look for a partner smart enough to make lots of money but stupid enough to give most of it to them.

857. A Hollywood star had just broken off her engagement to her wealthy fiance. "I saw him in a swim suit one day," she explained, "and he looked so different without his wallet."

858. "When I was a single girl," she said reflectively, "I said I would never marry a man who was bald, wore glasses or had artificial teeth. I didn't—but now he is, does, and has!"

859. There are two ways of achieving success: By putting your shoulder to the wheel or putting your head on the shoulder of the person at the wheel.

860. *Doris:* "When is your sister, Alice Ann, thinking of getting married?"
Little brother: "Constantly."

861. Accidentally meeting an acquaintance after several years, a girl said, "I never imagined you'd marry the man you did."
"Neither did I," replied the other. "I disliked his ways but I adored his means."

862. "I spent $50,000 on my daughter's education, and you want to marry her on an income of $20,000 a year!"
"Well, sir, that's forty per cent on your investment."

863. *Father:* "So you want to become my son-in-law, do you?"
Suitor: "No sir, I really don't. But I want to marry your daughter so I don't see how I can avoid it."

864. *Father:* "Jane, is that young man who is hanging around here so much really serious in his intentions?"
Daughter: "He must be. He wants to know how much I make, what kind of meals Mom serves, and if you two are easy to get along with."

865. The playful, middle-aged man sidled up to the young woman. "Where have you been all my life?" he asked.

She looked at him coolly and replied: "Well for the first half of it, I wasn't born!"

866. "Mother," said the teenage daughter, "what's the name of the boy I met on my vacation?"

"Which one, dear?" mother asked.

"You know, the one I couldn't live without."

867. One convict told his cellmate that a very nice thing had happened in the prison in which they were inmates—the warden's daughter had just married one of the cons who was serving a life term. And the warden was a little upset—because they had eloped.

868. "We are going to have a swell time tonight," the boy friend suggested. "I've got three seats for the theatre."

"Why do we need three seats?" she asked.

"They're for your father, mother, and kid brother," he said.

869. A young woman gave up her job as a secretary to marry an oil tycoon.

"He's the man I've always dreamed would one day come along and win me," she confided to her girl friends. "He's tall, dark—and has some."

870. The young man was rather shy, and after she had thrown her arms around him and kissed him for bringing her a bouquet of flowers, he jumped up and grabbed his hat.

"Oh, don't go," she said, as he made for the door. "I didn't mean to offend you."

"Oh, I'm not offended," he replied. "I'm going for more flowers."

871. A man who had been keeping company with a girl for several years took her to a Chinese restaurant. Studying the menu, he asked, "How would you like your rice—fried or boiled?"

Looking him straight in the eye, she replied, "Thrown."

872. A young prep-school lad is trying to decipher the following letter from his current girl friend: "Dear John, I hope

ROMANCE

you are not still angry. I want to explain that I was really joking when I told you I didn't mean what I said about reconsidering my decision not to change my mind. Please believe I really mean this. Love, Grace."

873. Stressing the importance of a large vocabulary, the English teacher told his class, "Use a word ten times and it will be yours for life."

In the back of the room a young girl closed her eyes and was heard chanting under her breath: "Fred, Fred, Fred, Fred, Fred, Fred, Fred, Fred, Fred, Fred."

874. "Why is it that you go steady with the girl?"
"Well, because she's different from other girls, I guess."
"How's that? In what way is she different?"
"She'll go with me."

875. She suddenly had an urge to live in the past. "You used to kiss me." So he leaned over and kissed her. "You used to hold my hand." So he reached out and held her hand. "You used to bite me on the back of the neck." He got up and walked out of the room.

"Where are you going?"
"To get my teeth."

876. "Thought you were going to visit your new girlfriend at her apartment tonight."
"I did."
"How come you're home so early?"
"Well, we sat awhile and chatted. Then, suddenly, she turned out the lights. I can take a hint."

S

Safety first

877. Flying to Los Angeles from San Francisco the other day, a passenger noticed that the "Fasten Seat Belts" sign was kept lit during the whole journey although the flight was a particularly smooth one.

Just before landing, he asked the stewardess about it.

"Well," explained the girl, "up front there are 17 University of California girls going to Los Angeles for the weekend. In back, there are 25 Coast Guard enlistees. What would you do?"

878. A man phoned the local fire station one night and asked, "Is this the Fire Department?"

"Yes," he was told.

"Listen," said the man. "I've just moved here, and I've spent a lot on the garden. I engaged men to . . ."

"Where's the fire?" interrupted the officer at the station.

". . . dig out the old stuff and lay out new lawns and beds. The lawn alone set me back . . ."

"Is your house on fire?" yelled the officer.

"No," the man said, "but the one next door is, and if anybody gets in touch with you about it, I don't want clodhoppin' firefighters draggin' hoses all over my new garden, see?"

Salary. See Wages

Sales

879. A high-pressured auto dealer told his customer, "Do you realize that, while you're standing here dickering, your car is depreciating?"

880. A shoe salesperson who had dragged out half her stock for a customer, said: "Mind if I rest a few minutes? Your feet are killing me!"

881. There's nothing quite as pathetic looking in a hotel dining room as a salesperson with an unlimited expense account and with ulcers.

882. *Customer:* "To what do you owe your extraordinary success as a house-to-house salesperson?"

Salesperson: "To the first five words I utter when a woman opens the door: 'Miss, is your mother in?' "

883. The new sales manager had called the sales force together and was laying down the law. "There's going to be a new regime around here—all work. And," he concluded, "from now on, I want you out of here and calling on your customers at the stroke of 9."

The salesperson next to me, always the wise guy, piped up, "The first stroke of 9 or the last stroke, sir?"

884. A persistent salesperson refused to leave when the secretary told him the boss was out. An hour passed, then two. Finally, weary of being a prisoner in her own office, the boss admitted the salesperson.

"My secretary told you I was out," exclaimed the puzzled boss. "How'd you know I was in?"

"Easy," explained the salesperson. "Your secretary was working."

885. Marshall Field, the merchant prince, once chided one of his department heads for stocking a fine Italian tablecloth. "You will never sell that in Chicago," he forecast.

A few weeks later the merchant dropped by to see his executive. "Barton," he said, "I owe you an apology. You did sell that tablecloth; I dined from it last night in a north side home."

"Yes," agreed the department head, "but your host returned it this morning for credit."

886. A second-hand car dealer having made a quick sale earlier was alarmed to see the purchaser driving back into his yard.

"Nothing wrong is there?"

"Not yet—I just wanted to return some things the previous owner, that quiet little titled lady, left in the car—her tobacco pouch in the glove locker and a bottle of Scotch under the seat!"

887. An itinerant salesperson for a children's encyclopedia was concluding a highly-charged sales talk. As the young mother hesitated, he turned to her five-year-old son and said, "Ask me a question, sonny. Ask me anything you want to know and I will show your mother where she can find the answer in this wonderful book."

The salesperson is working on another street now. The question the boy asked was, "What kind of a car does God drive?"

888. A small businessowner was in trouble with her sales. She decided to call in an expert to give her an outsider's viewpoint. After she had gone over her plans and problems, the businessowner took the sales expert to a map on the wall and showed him brightly colored pins stuck wherever she had a salesperson.

"Now," she asked the expert, "for a starter, what is the first thing we should do?"

"Well," replied the expert, "the first thing is to take those pins out of the map and stick them in the salespeople."

889. The sales manager was praising the efficiency of his organization at a banquet.

"We're now making a sale every three minutes," he announced proudly.

"That's not enough," came a voice from the audience.

The speaker paid no attention to the rude interruption but went on to tell of the new sales promotion and direct-mail campaign which would insure a sale every minute and a half.

"That's still not enough," the voice repeated.

Enraged, the speaker singled out the man who had spoken and barked, "You interrupted me twice. Now I wish you'd explain your remark."

"Certainly," came the reply, "there's a sucker born every minute."

890. A sports enthusiast rented a dog at a hunting lodge and had wonderful luck with him. A month later he went back and described the dog he wanted because he had forgotten to ask its name.

"Oh, you want Seller," beamed the lodge owner. "We've raised his rate from $25 to $50."

The hunter took the dog out anyway and enjoyed another fine day. When he went back the following month, he asked for Seller. The lodge owner explained that the dog was now called "Super Seller" and cost $75. The hunter took him out just the same, insisting he was well worth the money.

The next month when the hunter drove up in his car, the lodge owner greeted him with a sad smile. He said, "You can't have your favorite dog this time. A few days ago we made the mistake of naming him 'Sales Manager.' Now, all he will do is sit on his tail and bark."

891. An insurance representative was called on by the president of the company to report on the technique she used to sell a one million dollar policy.

Addressing her cohorts, the ace began: "I followed the rule book. When I got to his office, knowing what sticklers doctors are, I made sure to arrive on the button for our appointment. But the place was jammed. I waited four hours to see him, and he appreciated it. He told me that it was a pleasure to meet a salesperson who knows how to conduct herself in a professional office. I smiled, warmly, let him know that it was quite all right, and used this cue to ask him about himself. I listened attentively to every word, going out of my way to agree with the wonderful opinion he had of himself. He talked three hours, then asked me to come back. I did the next week, went through the same procedures, made the sale, and when I left his office I knew I'd made a friend for life." Then, after a pause, she concluded: "But boy!! What an enemy *he* made."

892. An incident involving U.S. Government officials in the early 1900s has a modern-day application. Uncle Joe Cannon, once the czar-like Speaker of the House of Representatives, announced one summer that he would take a party of friends through Yellowstone National Park. That was the opportunity for which Hiram Martin Chittenden had been waiting. Mr. Chittenden was the builder of the park road system.

There were four stagecoaches ready for Uncle Joe and his party. When the guests turned up, Chittenden arranged to have Uncle Joe placed in the last coach. The driver was instructed to keep as close to the coach ahead as he could without inviting disaster.

What a powdering Uncle Joe took back there! He was white with volcanic dust.

"Why in the devil," he rasped, "doesn't somebody do something about those blankety-blank roads?"

Chittenden, in a gentle voice, reminded him that there were plans drawn up but that there was no money available.

"Well, let's see the plans," ordered Mr. Cannon.

And out of the next Congress came $350,000 for the next three years, 1902-1905.

893.   Ben Holden in his column tells the story of a newly hired traveling salesperson named Gooch who wrote his first report to the home office. It stunned the brass in the sales department because it was obvious the new man was illiterate. Here is what he wrote . . .

"Dear Bos-

I have seen this outfit which ain't never bot a dimes worth of nothing from us and I sole them a couple hunerd thousand dollars of guds. I am now going to Chicawgo."

Before the illiterate could be given the heave-ho by the sales manager, this letter came from Chicago:

"I cum hear and sole them haff a millyon."

Fearful if he did and fearful if he didn't fire the illiterate, the sales manager dumped the problem in the lap of the president.

The following morning the staff in the ivory tower was amazed to see the two letters posted on the bulletin board, and this memo from the president above:

"To All Salespeople: We ben spending two much time trying to spel insted of trying to sel. Let's watch thoes sails. I want everybody shud reed these leters from Gooch, who is on the rode doin a grate job for us, and you shud go out and do like he done."

894.   One seasoned sales representative became increasingly concerned and frustrated with an overdue account. As a last ditch effort, she forwarded the following collection note: "Your business is appreciated, but enough is enough. Your account is now ten months over due. That means we have carried you longer than your mother did. Immediate delivery is expected."

School

895.   Peter did not have a very successful school experience. In fact, before he could attend his ten-year high school reunion, his principal made him take a make-up exam.

896.   Many of Mary's friends graduated Cum Laude or Summa Cum Laude. As she received her diploma, a professor could be heard saying, "Laude, how come we're letting her graduate."

897.   A successful salesperson now found himself in the top 10% of his company's salesforce. "That's quite an accomplishment for me," he said. "When I was in college, I graduated in the half of the class that made the upper half possible."

898.   It is a lonely experience to run for freshman class president and lose—two years in a row.

899.   Jimmy managed to develop the reputation of being the class rowdy. The situation worsened every year until finally his parents began attending PTA meetings under an assumed last name.

900.   John struggled through his college years but was able to graduate in four terms . . . those were the Johnson, Nixon, Ford, and Carter presidential terms.

Season—Seasons

901.   Have you heard about the self-made millionaire who winters in Florida, summers in Maine, falls for the opposite sex and springs at the thought of marriage?

902.   "The weather here in Florida is wonderful," said the retired lady. "How do you tell summer from winter?"

Replied the hotel clerk: "In winter we get Cadillacs, Lincolns and stuffed shirts. In summer we get Chevrolets, Fords and stuffed shorts."

Secrecy

903. "What is the difference between a secret and a public session of the town council?"

"When there is a secret session, one knows the result an hour later; the result of a public session, one reads in the next day's paper."

Secretary—Secretaries

904. *Advice to office help:* "Take your shorthand at arm's length."

Self-concept

905. A man with a low self-concept had difficulty asking women out. When he finally did work up the nerve, the potential date responded with a flat "NO!"

"That's OK," he responded, "I really can't blame you." Then he started thinking, "If this is all the better she can do, I don't want to go out with her anyway."

906. Conceit would be OK if only the right people had it.

Self-confidence

907. A college professor, telling a student that there was no excuse for his poor spelling, said: "You should consult a dictionary whenever you are in doubt. It's as simple as that."

The student appeared confused. "But," he replied, "I'm never in doubt."

908. While stopping at a New England hotel, a high-pressured New York executive was suddenly taken ill. The elderly physician who attended him was much too deliberate for his taste. "Don't know why I'm letting you take care of me in the first place," snapped the executive. "Guess I just have a lot of faith in fools."

"Yup," replied the seasoned doctor agreeably. "I can see you have a remarkable amount of self-confidence."

Semantics

909. *Bishop (reading telegram from one of his ministers):* "My wife passed away Wednesday. Please send substitute for over the weekend."

Sharing

910. The bus was already crowded when a rather large woman entered. She stood for a moment glaring at the seated passengers. "Isn't some gentleman going to offer me a seat" she asked.

At this, one exceptionally small man rose. "Well," he said, rather shyly, "I'm willing to make a contribution."

Silence

911. One way to save face is to keep the lower half shut.

912. "Your boy friend stayed very late last night, didn't he?"

"Yes, mother, did the noise disturb you?"

"No, but the periods of silence did."

913. At a dinner party, the subject of eternal life and future punishment came up for a lengthy discussion.

Mark Twain took no part in it, so the woman seated next to him asked: "Why haven't you said something? Surely you must have some opinion about this."

"Madam, you must excuse me," Twain replied. "I am silent because of necessity. I have friends in both places."

914. The story is told that when Western Union offered to buy the ticker invented by Thomas Edison, the great inventor was unable to name a price. Edison asked for a couple of days to consider it. Talking the matter over with his wife, she suggested he ask $20,000, but this seemed exorbitant to Edison. At the appointed time, Edison returned to the Western Union office. He was asked to name his price. "How much?" asked the Western Union official. Edison tried to say $20,000, but lacked the courage, and just stood there speechless.

The official waited a moment, then broke the silence and said, "Well, how about $100,000?"

Sin

915. A preacher recently announced that there are 726 different kinds of sin. He is now being besieged with requests for the list, mostly from people who think they are missing something.

916. The pastor was rejoicing with a little old lady over one of her elderly relatives, who had finally seen the light and joined the church after a lifetime of riotous living.

When she wondered if all the oldster's carryings-on would be forgiven, the pastor assured her, "Yes, indeed, the greater the sinner, the greater the saint."

"Preacher," she mused wistfully. "I wish I had learned this forty years ago."

Size

917. George Washington Carver, the scientist who achieved wonders with the humble peanut, used to tell this story:

When I was young I said to God, "God, tell me the mystery of the universe." But God answered, "That knowledge is reserved for Me alone." So I said, "God tell me the mystery of the peanut." Then God said, "Well, George, that's more nearly your size." And He told me.

918. A man walked into a pet shop, pointed to a large dog in a kennel and said:

"How much do you want for that big dog?"

"Fifty dollars," replied the clerk.

"And how much for that small fellow over there?" asked the customer.

"One hundred dollars," was the reply.

"And for that tiny one?"

"Two hundred dollars," said the clerk.

The customer looked puzzled.

"How much," he asked, "will it cost me if I don't buy a dog at all?"

Smoking

919.   "Sir," said the intrusive lady to a stranger seated next to her on the train, "smoking makes me sick."

"Well, then, madam," replied the stranger, "if I were you I'd give it up."

920.   On her son's seventeenth birthday a mother pleadingly asked, "Promise me you'll tell me when you start smoking. Don't let me find it out from the neighbors."

"Don't worry about me, Mom," the son replied. "I quit smoking a year ago."

921.   The visitor turned to the hostess and said, "My, this is a fancy vase on your mantel. What's this in it?"

"My husband's ashes," she replied.

"Oh, I'm sorry," said the visitor. "How long has he been dead?"

"Oh, he's not dead," said the wife. "He's just too lazy to find an ashtray."

922.   A young preacher spoke adamantly against the sins of the world. Among other things to which he objected was smoking. One day he saw a parishioner enjoying an after-dinner smoke on his pipe.

"Hey Joe," he said, "when your time comes to go and you apply for admission at the gate of Heaven, do you expect that St. Peter will let you in if he detects the odor of tobacco on your breath?"

The man took the pipe out of his mouth and said: "Young man, when I go to Heaven I expect to leave my breath behind."

Speaking

923.   Why is it listeners always know when the speaker should stop and he seldom does?

Malcolm S. Forbes

924. The following announcement was printed in a bulletin of the LaGrave Avenue Christian Reformed Church in Grand Rapids, Michigan: "Someone has taken the paper-cutter from the church office. We are in dire need of its immediate return. Please bear in mind that without our paper-cutter, the sermons will get longer."

925. "How was my first sermon, Granny?" asked the young minister. He knew she'd tell the truth.

"I saw only three things wrong with it," mused the frank old lady.

"Only three things wrong . . . not bad for my first attempt," said the young man excitedly. "What were they?" he asked.

"Well!" drawled the grandmother. "First, you read it! Second, you didn't read it well! And third, it wasn't worth reading anyhow!"[3]

926. As Cardinal Cushing delivered the invocation at President Kennedy's inauguration, an accident near the podium caused billows of smoke to rise. One of the reporters, seated near the incident, turned to a colleague and commented, "Boy, when the Cardinal is hot, he's really hot."

927. William Evarts, a 19th Century Secretary of State, enjoyed the reputation of being an entertaining after-dinner speaker. Asked to give a few comments at a holiday banquet, he rose to the podium and began, "You have been enjoying a turkey stuffed with sage and now I trust you will enjoy this sage stuffed with turkey."

928. Before I speak, I have something important to say.
Groucho Marx

929. Legend has it that once upon a time a tiger ate a bull. The tiger was so satisfied with his feast that he growled and growled. A big game hunter heard the growling, tracked it to the tiger, and with one shot, killed him.

Moral: When you are full of bull, keep your mouth shut.

---

[3] Nido R. Qubein, *Communicate Like a Pro*, Prentice-Hall, Inc., Englewood Cliffs, New Jersey, 1983, page 163.

930. A public speaker was invited to address the Alumni Association at Yale University. Admonished to keep his comments brief, the speaker decided to base his speech on the four letters that spell YALE. He began by saying that the letter Y stands for Youth—young people who come to the university filled with potential. The A, he continued, stands for Attitude—the desire to learn and grow.

After lengthy remarks on the Y and A, he moved on to L, pointing out that it stood for Loyalty—the devotion necessary for alumni to possess toward their alma mater. The thought was good but the speaker rambled on for quite some time concerning this point. Finally, he came to his last letter. E, he said, is for Enthusiasm—the feeling everyone here has about being a Yale graduate.

An hour and a half later, the speaker concluded. As he sat down, a bored listener whispered to his neighbor, "I'm sure glad we didn't graduate from Southern Methodist University."

931. A city council person was making an impassioned speech urging city leaders to vote yes on a controversial community betterment project. His wrap-up, intended to inspire a commitment to action, drew a room full of laughter as he thundered: "We must grasp the bull by the tail, and look the matter squarely in the face!"

932. "As I left Denver to come here today," began a corporate president, "my secretary gave me a few words of encouragement. She said, 'I know you're nervous about addressing the field staff but don't be intimidated. And don't try to be charming, intellectual, or funny. Just be yourself.'"

933. "My keynote address was an entire flop," a speaker lamented to her husband. "Every time I was about to make a major point, someone would yell out 'up in front.'"

Space, Outer. See Outer space

Specialization

934. *Naive Student:* "Why, sir, what kind of a doctor are you?" *Officer:* "I'm a naval surgeon."
Student: "Goodness, how you doctors do specialize."

Spelling

935. *School term report card:* "Your son's handwriting is so bad we cannot tell whether he can spell or not."

936. The nice thing about dictating letters is that you can use a lot of words you don't know how to spell.

937. *Secretary:* "Sometimes I think our boss is a jerk. He told me to cross one of the 't's' out of 'rabbitt' but didn't say which one."

938. *Daughter:* "Oh, mother, I took Henry into the loving room last night and . . ."
Mother: "That's *living*, dear . . ."
Daughter: "You're telling me."

939. The examination question was a real puzzler. It asked why "psychic" is spelled with a "p".
The young student in the far corner did not have the answer, but he felt he should not leave the question unheeded. Shaking his head, he wrote, "It pcertainly does pseem psilly."

940. "I think," said the less-than-competent typist to her friend, "that the boss has decided to keep me."
"Has he said anything?"
"No. But this morning he gave me a dictionary."

941. A man picked up the phone and dialed the operator. His connection was completed and he told the operator: "I want to place a call to Pottawatomie, Indiana."
"Please spell it," the clerk said.
"Listen, lady," the man said, "if I could spell it, I wouldn't call—I'd write a letter."

Sports

942. Just as the trio of baseball umpires was walking onto the field before a big crowd, the band struck up the embarrassing tune, "Three Blind Mice."

943. A Russian track coach, interviewed by an American sportswriter, was asked why the Soviets are now producing such fast runners.

"It's really quite simple," the coach replied. "We use real bullets in our starting guns."

944. Two old ladies decided to take in one of the bowl games on New Year's Day. They watched the kickoff and the various plays throughout a scoreless first half.

When the teams lined up for the second-half kickoff, one of them turned to the other and said, "It's time to go home. This is where we came in."

945. A minister walked through the lobby of a hotel one morning and noticed a ballplayer he knew by sight. So he sauntered over to the player and introduced himself and said: "One thing I've always wondered. Why must you play ball on Sunday?"

"Well, Reverend," smiled the player, "Sunday is our biggest day—we get the best crowds—take in more money—and after all, Sunday is your biggest day, too, isn't it?"

There was a nod of understanding, but the minister explained: "But there's a little difference. You see, I'm in the right field." The player brightened and responded eagerly: "So am I, and ain't the sun hell out there?"

Status quo

946. A woebegone-looking adventurer reached the riverside, and approached the old captain who operated the ferry across the stream. "Dad," he whined, "I'm broke and have to get across the river. Will you trust me for it?"

"Fare's only a dollar," said the ferryman.

"I know it, but I haven't got a nickel to my name," explained the traveler.

The old captain took a puff at his pipe. "Well, mister," he said, "if you ain't got a nickel you won't be no better off on the other side than you are here."

Stinginess

947. "Did you read in the paper where old Andy McAndrews has left a quarter of a million dollars?"

"That old miser didn't leave a penny! He was *separated* from it."

Stubbornness

948. A couple traveled several miles down a country highway in silence. An earlier argument left both unwilling to concede their positions. Passing a barnyard of mules, the husband sarcastically asked, "Are they relatives of yours?"

"Yes," his wife replied. "I married into the family."

Surprise

949. "I told her I wanted to be surprised for dinner, so she soaked the labels off the cans."

950. The lady in the bathtub heard a knock at the front door.

"Who's there?" she called out.

"A blind salesperson," came the answer.

Thinking it would be entirely proper, she went to the door as she was. A young man stepped inside with: "Here's the blinds you ordered. Where shall I put 'em?"

951. A middle-aged man set off for a house where a children's party had been arranged. "Don't announce me," he said to the man who let him in.

Leaving his hat and coat in the hall, he opened the family room door, through which a buzz of conversation could be heard. Dropping on his hands and knees, he entered making noises like a horse neighing.

There was a dead silence. He looked up and found half a dozen people regarding him with perplexity and alarm. He was in the wrong house.

Surprises

952. A mother of twelve was asked, "What is the worst thing you could get on your twenty-fifth wedding anniversary?"

"Morning sickness," she replied.

Suspense

953. A film actor took his wife to the hospital for the birth of their first child. For the purpose of the film on which he had been working, the father-to-be sported a two-weeks' growth of very dark beard. While waiting anxiously, he was joined by another expectant father—a haggard young man who paced the floor for several minutes before noticing the first man sitting in a corner. When he did spot him, the young man turned pale.

"Good heavens!" he said. "How long have you been waiting?"

Suspicion

954. Interviewing a woman applicant, a kindly Social Security claims representative wanted to make sure that no tangles would prevent her from getting her full benefits. "Were either you or your husband married before?" he asked.

The woman glared indignantly and snapped: "Before what?"

955. "I don't like to pry into your affairs," said the lady to her husband. "But something's been bothering me for days."

"So?" said the husband. "Tell me all about it."

"You got a letter last Friday," the lady said. "It was perfumed. It was in a girl's handwriting. I saw you open it; you broke into a sweat. You turned white. Your hands trembled . . . For goodness' sake, who was it from and what did it say?"

"Oh, that," said the husband. "I decided it was best for both of us not to talk about it at the time. I've been trying to think of the best way of discussing it with you without causing an explosion."

"For heaven's sake," screamed the woman. "Tell me who it was from and what it said."

"Okay," said the husband. "It was from your dress shop. It said you owe them $740."

T

Table-turning

956. *Patient to dentist:* "This may hurt a little. I don't have the money."

957. Henry Ward Beecher, famous New England minister, was opening his mail one morning. Drawing a single sheet of paper from an envelope, he found written on it the one word: *Fool.*

The next Sunday, in the course of his sermon, he referred to it in these words: "I have known many an instance of a man writing letters and forgetting to sign his name. But this is the only instance I've ever known of a man signing his name and forgetting to write his letter."

Tact

958. When a prominent clergy was asked his opinion of advertising in America, he hesitated to make any comment on advertising itself, but he did offer to pray for the people who made a living at it.

959. A noted French statesperson was in the habit of bluntly speaking his mind, much to the dismay of his political advisers.

"You must be more tactful," they urged him. "Your strong language only makes you enemies."

The politician couldn't see it that way.

"It also makes me friends," he argued. "I have as my supporters all the enemies of my enemies."

960. The captain approached the sergeant with a bit of bad news. "Sergeant," he said, "we just got notice that Smith's grandmother died. You'd better go break the news to him."

The sergeant walked into the barracks, paused at the doorway and shouted, "Hey, Smith, your grandmother died."

The captain was horrified. "Sergeant, that's no way to tell a man that his grandmother has died. Look how you've shocked him. You have to use tact in a situation like this. I think we'd better send you to Tact and Diplomacy School."

So the sergeant spent a year studying at Tact and Diplomacy School. On the day he returned, the captain approached him.

"Well, sergeant, how did you do in school?"

"Fine," replied the sergeant. "I've really learned how to be tactful."

"That's good, because we've just gotten notice that Lopez's grandmother died. Go in and tell him."

The sergeant entered the barracks, paused at the doorway and called his men to attention. When they were lined up he stepped before them and ordered, "All those with living grandmothers step forward. Not so fast, Lopez."

Talkativeness. See Loquacity

Tardiness

961. *Steno to irate boss:* "Certainly I have a good reason for being late! It makes the day seem shorter!"

962. *Boss:* "You're twenty-five minutes late, young man. Don't you know what time our people start to work around here?" *Teen-age employee:* "No, sir. They're always at it when I get here."

Taxation

963. Taxation, like a lot of other things, is based on supply and demand. The Government demands, and we supply.

964. A transfer student in a night-school English class was disturbed when the instructor announced: "Tomorrow night we will take up syntax."

"Goodness!" she exclaimed. "If they're going to collect *that*, I'll never be able to afford the tuition."

Taxes

965. There's this to be said about taxes—if the taxpayer is alive, he's kicking.

966. *This sign on a New York service station:* "We collect taxes—federal, state, and local. We also sell gasoline as a sideline."

967. The biggest job Congress has is how to get the money from the taxpayer without disturbing the voter.

968. Two people were discussing the high rate of taxes and government waste of money. Just then a school bus passed them. "See what I mean," exclaimed one. "When I was a boy we walked three miles to school and three miles back home each day. Now we spend $5,000 for a bus to pick up the children so they don't have to walk. Then we spend $50,000 for a gymnasium so they can get exercise."

969. Once, when William Gladstone was Britain's Chancellor of the Exchequer, he attended a lecture given by Michael Faraday, the physicist. When it was over, Gladstone said to the scientist: "What you spoke about is purely theoretical, but does it have any practical value?"

"What do you mean by 'practical value'?" asked Faraday.

"I mean," replied Gladstone, "can it be taxed?"

970. The Internal Revenue Service has developed a "new, simplified," tax form. Preparers need answer only three questions:
1. How much money did you make last year?
2. How much money do you have left?
3. Send the amount listed for question #2.

971. The State of Michigan instituted new tax forms that immediately received public criticism. The forms contained numerous misspelled words and this "new, simplified version" appeared more difficult to complete than the previous form. One

Michigan resident said the new tax forms resembled a secret government IQ test.

Teacher—Pupil

972.   Somebody has said that payola started when the first kid gave his teacher an apple.

973.   *History teacher:* "Johnny, name the addresses we best remember Washington and Lincoln by."
Johnny: "Mount Vernon and Springfield."

974.   "What did you do in school?" a mother asked her little girl when she returned from her first academic day.
"Nothing," the girl replied. "Some woman wanted to know how to spell 'cat', and I told her."

975.   To stimulate her young pupils, a first-grade teacher arranged to take her class on an "educational tour" of a farmyard. But one small boy saw right through her scheme. "Don't look, don't look!" he warned his buddy. "If we look we'll have to tell about it tomorrow!"

976.   *Teacher (pointing at a deer in the zoo):* "Johnny, what is that?"
Johnny: "I don't know."
Teacher: "What does your mother call your father?"
Johnny: "Don't tell me that's a louse."

977.   One day a teacher asked her first-graders what they did to help at home. They took turns giving such answers as, "I dry dishes," "I feed the dog," and "I make my bed." Then she noticed that Johnny hadn't spoken, so she asked him to tell what he did.
After hesitating a moment, he replied: "Mostly, I stay out of the way."

978.   *Teacher:* "Which is more important to us—the moon or the sun?"
Pupil: "The moon."
Teacher: "Why?"
Pupil: "The moon gives us light at night when we need it. The sun gives us light only in the daytime when we don't need it."

979. *Teacher:* "Give me a sentence with an 'object' in it."
Pupil: "Teacher, you're the most wonderful and beautiful lady I've ever seen."
Teacher: "Thanks, but what's the 'object'?"
Pupil: "I'd like to go home a little earlier today."

980. "Now, how many of you would like to go to heaven?" asked the Sunday school teacher. All the eager three-year-olds raised their hands except Tommy.

"I'm sorry, I can't. My mother told me to come right home after Sunday school."

Technique

981. "Joe," a friend asked a young businessman, "how do you expect to accomplish anything at your office with three good-looking typists around?"

"Easy," was the confident answer. "I'll give two of them the same day off."

982. "Begin your story well," a famous author once counseled a group of budding writers. "It's half the battle. Always bear in mind," he continued, "the case of the young man, who desiring to marry, obtained a favorable hearing from his sweetheart's father by opening the interview with the words: 'I know a way, sir, whereby you can save a lot of money.' "

Teenage

983. The teller at the deposit window of the bank sharply reprimanded a man because he had neither filled out a deposit slip nor put his loose silver in the special little rolls of specified amounts.

"When you've done this properly, I'll be glad to accept your deposit," said the teller curtly.

The man accepted this tirade meekly and went to a counter to follow instructions. When he returned later to the window the teller half-apologized.

"Oh, that's all right," said the man graciously. "I have a houseful of teenagers, so I'm used to being spoken to as if I don't do anything right."

Telephone

984. The bathtub was invented in 1850, and the telephone in 1875. Had you lived in 1850, you could have sat in the bathtub for the next 25 years without having the phone ring once.

985. In the business world an executive knows something about everything, a technician knows everything about something—and the switchboard operator knows everything.

986. "Who was that on the telephone?" the man of the house asked his new maid.

"I dunno," she answered. "Someone just said, 'Long distance from New York.' So I said 'Yes, it certainly is' and hung up."

987. A telephone repair person, who had just installed some new equipment in the Pentagon, started to leave but became lost in the maze that has driven many a visitor to despair.

Finally, in a claustrophobic state, he ducked into an office and called to the switchboard operator:

"How in the devil do I get outside?"

"Just dial 9," snapped the operator busily.

988. "This is Perkins, Potter, Parker and Potts, good morning."

"Is Mr. Potter there?"

"May I ask who is calling?"

"This is Mr. Sullivan's office, of Sullivan, Chadwick, Bicknell and Jones."

"Just a moment, I'll connect you."

"Mr. Potter's office."

"Mr. Potter, please. Mr. Sullivan wants him."

"Will you put Mr. Sullivan on the line please"

"Mr. Sullivan? Ready with Mr. Potter."

"Hello, Pete? This is Joe. Okay for lunch? Good! See you."

Television

989. A lady phoned her TV service repairer and complained that something was wrong with her set. The service person asked her if there were any visible symptoms.

"The newscaster is on right now," said the lady, "and he has a very long face."

"Madam," replied the technician, "if you had to report what's happening these days you'd have a long face too."

990. A rating service learned that it inadvertently obtained part of its findings from prisoners in the same compound. They also discovered that the prisoners were only watching daytime TV.

Unable to resist its natural urge, the rating outfit asked the prisoners why they never watched at night.

"That's simple," explained a prisoner. "The lights go out at 8:00 and we are not allowed to watch after that."

"But why do you watch it during the daytime?" persisted the prober.

"I thought it was part of the punishment," replied the prisoner.

Theft

991. Some of us who talk too much at times may learn something from the mistake made by Rastus.

Judge: "Guilty, or not guilty?"

Rastus: "Not guilty, sir."

Judge: "Have you ever been in jail?"

Rastus: "No, sir, I never stole nothin' before."

Thrift

992. The best thing to save for your old age is yourself.

993. The young couple walked into a car dealer's showroom and was taken aback by the suggested price of a compact car.

"But that's almost the cost of a big car," the husband said.

"Well," said the salesperson, "if you want economy, you got to pay for it."

994. An old farmer was once asked by a young man how it was he had become so rich.

"It is a long story," said the old man, "and while I'm telling it we may as well save the candle." And he put it out.

"You need not tell the story," said the youth. "I understand."

995. A University of British Columbia professor who makes almost a ritual of walking to work, rain or shine, consented to accept a lift from a friend who overtook him hiking along through a heavier-than-usual coastal mist.

As the professor climbed in, the driver noticed he wore only one rubber and exclaimed sympathetically, "Lost a rubber, huh?" When the professor merely answered no, his friend demanded, "Isn't it a bit odd wearing only one?"

The professor said no again, adding, "Only one shoe has a hole in it."

Tip—Tips—Tipping

996. "I will take a meal out occasionally but I never get to the same restaurant twice," a man remarked. To which his friend quickly replied: "I don't ever leave a tip either."

997. *From Miami Beach:* "Bellhop, can I get change for a dollar?"

"Lady, at this hotel, a dollar is change."

998. "Your son tips me more generously than you do, sir," said the taxi driver.

"That's quite possible. He has a wealthy father. I haven't."

999. The homeowner was delighted with the way the painter had decorated his house.

"You did a fine job," he said, "and I'm going to give you a little something extra. Here's $20. Take the Mrs. to a show."

That night the bell rang and the painter stood at the door, all dressed up.

"What is it," the man asked, "did you forget something?"

"No," replied the painter. "I just came to take the missus to a show."

1000. A millionaire speculator developed a reputation for being a lavish tipper. Ironically, this resulted at times in poorer service.

He particularly liked bellhops. At one time, when he was stopping at a New York hotel, he instructed his secretary to tip them $1.00 for any service, no matter how trivial.

After a few weeks, it struck him that he must be getting a staggering amount of service, as the tips were running into several hundred dollars a week. His heavy mail, about 100 letters a day, was being brought up with something less than promptness.

Finally, he put two and two together and made an investigation. Sure enough, he discovered that the mail was being delivered one letter at a time.

Tit for Tat

1001. *Man to neighbor:* "Let's make a deal. I'll stop keeping up with you, if you'll stop keeping up with me."

1002. A wise teacher sent this note home at the start of the term: "If you promise not to believe everything your children say happens at school, I'll promise not to believe everything they say happens at home."

1003. The wife was crying at her daughter's wedding. Her husband consoled her with the following: "Don't think of it as losing a daughter. Think of it as gaining a bathroom."

1004. "I'm sorry if our hammering disturbed you. We were hanging a picture."

"Oh, that's perfectly all right. I just came over to ask if it was okay if we hung a picture on the other end of the nail."

1005. A southern senator once pointed to a drove of mules just in from Ohio and said to a senator friend: "There go some of your constituents."

"Yes," said the Ohio senator gravely. "They are on their way down South to teach school."

1006. *John:* "My wife had an argument with the electric company."

Jim: "Who won?"

John: "It was a tie. We don't get any electricity, and they don't get any money."

1007. "Dear Alice," wrote the young man, "I'm getting so forgetful, that while I remember proposing to you last night, I forgot whether you said 'Yes' or 'No'."

"Dear Bob," Alice replied, "so glad to hear from you. I knew I said 'No' to someone last night, but I had forgotten just who it was."

1008. Parson Webster phoned the local board of health to ask that a dead mule be removed from in front of his house. The young clerk who answered thought he'd be smart.

"I thought you ministers took care of the dead," he wisecracked.

"We do," answered the parson, "but first we get in touch with their relatives."

1009. "How do you do, my dear?" said the elderly lady to the little girl.

"Quite well, thank you," was the polite reply.

There was a pause and then the lady asked, "Why don't you ask me how I am?"

"Because," said the child calmly, "I'm not interested."

1010. A native of Ireland applied for a job in a powder plant. "What can you do?" asked the supervisor.

"Anything, sar, just anything," replied the hopeful man.

"Well," drawled the supervisor, thinking to have some fun with the newcomer, "you seem to be all right. Could you wheel out a barrow of smoke?"

"Shure!" exclaimed the man. "Just fill it up for me!"

1011. A lady phoned the president of a large furniture store at 2 a.m. After long ringing, a sleepy, gruff voice answered.

"This is Miss Gruntled," said the lady in sugary tones. "I just had to call you personally to tell you that the couch I bought at your store last week is simply stunning."

"I'm delighted to hear it," yawned the president. "But why, may I ask, do you call me in the middle of the night about a couch you bought last week?"

"Because," she replied sweetly, "your truck just delivered it."

1012. Two counterfeiters with a talented but stupid engraver found themselves with a large quantity of almost-perfect bills on their hands. The trouble was, they were all $18 bills. The crooks decided to go far back into the hill country to dispose of the bills because "nobody up there sees much money." Deep in the mountains, they flashed one on a crossroads storekeeper and talked him into changing it.

"How do you want it?" he asked. "Would two sevens and a four be all right?"

1013. In *Healing Heart*, Norman Cousins relates a conflict he had some years ago with a telephone operator:

I went to the telephone to call the office and promptly lost a dime when an operator came on and asked for a quarter. It was a recording. I put in another dime, got a live operator, told her what happened, and she said the phone company would be glad to send me the dime if I would give her my name and address.

It seemed absurd that the phone company would spend 25 cents in stamps, to say nothing of personnel expense, just to refund a dime and I said so. I also pressed the coin-return lever.

At that point, all the innards of the machine opened up, and quarters and dimes tumbled out in magnificent profusion.

"Operator," I asked, "are you still there?"

"Yes."

"Operator, something quite remarkable has just happened. All I did was press the coin-return lever, and the machine is giving me all its earnings. There must be more than three dollars in coins here, and the flow hasn't stopped."

"Sir," she said, "will you please put the money back in the box?"

"Operator," I said, "if you will give me your name and address, I'll be glad to mail it to you."

Published by Norton

1014. The story is told of Eve Arden rehearsing her leading role in a stage production. With the rehearsal well underway, the phone on the stage rang. Realizing this was not part of the script, Arden was immediately taken back by the ringing phone. She glanced at the leading man, sensing he might have something to do with this surprise event. Arden answered the phone, listened for a moment, and then motioned to the leading man. "Here, it's for you," she said.

Traffic, Automobile

1015.   Some people have a wonderful sense of right and wrong, but little sense of right and left.

1016.   Air travel will be much safer when they eliminate the automobile ride between the city and the airport.

1017.   The automobile may have replaced the horse and buggy—but it's still wise for the drivers to stay on the wagon.

1018.   If you make a left turn from a right-hand lane, you are probably just careless or reckless and not at all what the driver behind called you.

Transformation, Religious

1019.   A party of clergy were attending a Presbyterian conference in Scotland. Several of them set off to explore the district. Presently they came to a river spanned by a temporary bridge. Not seeing the notice that said it was unsafe, they began to cross it. The bridge keeper ran after them in protest.

"It is all right," declared one of the ministers, not understanding the reason for the old man's haste, "we're Presbyterians from the conference."

"I'm no caring aboot that," was the reply, "but if ye dinna get off the bridge, you'll all be Baptists!"

Travel

1020.   There are only two ways to travel—first class and with children.

1021.   The best way to see America nowadays is to try to get your son, or daughter, into college.

1022.   People in big cities are not essentially rude. They are just afraid of being mistaken for visitors.

1023.   *Wife:* "I wish I could find a book to tell us where to go on a vacation this winter."

Husband: "We have one book to tell us where we can't go—our check book."

1024.   An American tourist stopped at an inn in a small French village and ordered a couple of scrambled eggs for lunch. Afterward he noted with astonishment that he had been charged five dollars apiece for them and asked, "Are eggs scarce here?"

"No, monsieur," said the innkeeper. "Eggs are plentiful. But Americans, they are scarce here."

1025.   A couple from New Haven, Connecticut, were driving through Maine in an attempt to discover their rich New England heritage.

When they stopped in front of the general store in a quaint old town, the visitor asked the proprietor what the town was noted for.

"Tourists," grunted the man sourly.

"But what do they raise here?"

The native eyed the young man with contempt and replied, "Hell."

1026.   An elderly couple was on their first jet airplane ride. At every stop on their cross-country adventure, the plane would land and the red fuel truck would drive out to refuel the big bird.

At Phoenix, Omaha, Chicago, and New York. . . each time the plane taxied up to the gate, the red fuel truck was close behind and would pull up beside it.

As the couple landed in Washington, D.C., the woman leaned back in her seat and sighed. "Just think," she said to her husband, "we just soared across the entire country at 600 miles per hour."

"Yes," replied her husband, "and did you notice that little red truck didn't do too bad either."

Trouble—Troubles

1027.   People are like tea bags. . . they don't know their own strength until they get into hot water.

1028.   The spouses of two prominent manufacturers were talking things over in the lobby of a hotel.

"Does your spouse confide business troubles to you?" asked one.

"Oh, yes, indeed," replied the other. "Every time I come home with something new!"

Truth

1029.   A piano manufacturer tried to get a testimonial from Will Rogers for his pianos. Rogers, who never endorsed any product unless he really believed in it, wrote this letter to the piano firm: "Dear Sirs: I guess your pianos are the best I ever leaned against. Yours truly, Will Rogers."

1030.   The wife of an art dealer, who was anxious to sell some Gothic tapestries to a renowned art lover, was amazed and annoyed when her husband awakened her at three o'clock one morning and commanded her to say, "I'll pay you a million dollars for your Gothic tapestries."

She could see no sense in that. In the first place, she didn't have a million dollars and even if she had, why should she offer to buy tapestries from her own husband?

"Just say it, please," he implored.

Sleepily she complied, repeated the suggested words, turned over and went back to sleep.

At nine o'clock the next morning the dealer, who took great pride in his integrity, told his potential buyer, "I can swear on a stack of Bibles that at three o'clock this morning I had an offer of a million dollars for those tapestries."

Turnabout

1031.   Then there was the one about the goose flying south for the winter who flew past a drive-in showing a horror movie and was so frightened he got people-pimples.

1032.   A Minneapolis man, convalescing after surgery, visited by his wife one evening, suggested a stroll. They wound up on the maternity floor, admiring the babies. While oohing and aahing, they heard muffled snickers, then realized the spectacle—the man in his hospital bathrobe, the woman in street clothes outside the nursery window.

1033. Sam, the private eye, was giving his client a report. "I trailed your husband into four bars and then to a bachelor's apartment," he said.

"Aha!" exclaimed the wife. "Go on, go on! What was he doing there?"

"Well, lady," Sam responded in an embarrassed tone, "near as I could make out, he was trailing you."

1034. The story is told that Abe Lincoln once rented a horse from a man who opposed him politically. The man provided Lincoln with a slow horse, hoping he would not arrive on time to deliver an important speech. Lincoln made it there, but on the way back, planned how to get back at the stable owner. As Lincoln turned in the horse, he innocently asked if this particular horse was reserved for funerals. Assured that such was not the case, Lincoln replied, "Well, I'm glad of that! If you did, he'd never get the corpse to the grave in time for the Resurrection!"

1035. One day, while browsing through the library of a neighbor, Mark Twain came across a book that appealed to him. He kindly asked the neighbor if he could borrow it for a few days.

"You're welcome to read it anytime you wish," the neighbor responded, "but you will have to read it here. You see, I have a rule that books cannot leave these premises."

A few weeks later, the neighbor was at Twain's door requesting to borrow his lawn mower. "Certainly," said Twain, "but according to my rule, you must use it on these premises."

Twins

1036. An impetuous student negotiated a date with a pair of Siamese twins one night.

"Have a good time?" asked his roommate later.

"Yes and No."

1037. Two young guys were discussing their conquests and the first young man reminisced rapturously about one of his former girl friends, mentioning that she was a twin.

"Twins?" his buddy queried. "How did you tell them apart?"

"Oh, that wasn't so hard. Her brother has a mustache!"

V

Vacation—Vacationing

1038. It was his first day back on the job after his vacation.

"How did you enjoy your trip?" asked a fellow worker.

"Well," sighed the weary traveler, "have you ever spent four days in a station wagon with those you thought you loved best?"

1039. One evening when Thomas Edison came home from work, his wife said to him, "You've worked long enough without a rest. You must go on a vacation."

"But where on earth would I go?" asked Mr. Edison.

"Just decide where you would rather be than anywhere else on earth," suggested the wife.

Mr. Edison hesitated. "Very well," he said finally, "I'll go tomorrow."

The next morning he was back at work in his laboratory.

1040. "Whenever we start a vacation," writes Robert Orben, "it's the same thing. We get up at six o'clock in the morning to get an early start. First we eat breakfast; then we pack; then we notify the neighbors and police department; then we stop the milk, mail, and newspaper deliveries; then we arrange for a kid to mow the lawn and water the garden; then we take the dog to the kennel; then the kids say goodbye to their friends; then we set the lights that go on automatically, activate the burglar alarm system, lock all the doors and windows—and after all this is finally done, you know what we do? We go to bed because I hate night driving!"

219

Value—Values

1041. A burglar gave his girl friend a fur coat. "It's wonderful," she exclaimed. "It must be worth at least ten years."

1042. A family had just moved to a small town in New England and after finding a house to live in, the woman of the family was familiarizing herself with the local stores. Intent on getting some meat for her family's evening meal, she entered the only meat market in the village and was surprised to find only two trays of meat in the showcase. Upon closer examination she found that the meat looked exactly alike to her.

"How much is this meat?" she asked, pointing to one of the cases.

"Two dollars a pound," replied the butcher.

"And that?" she asked, pointing to the other tray.

"Three dollars a pound," was his reply.

"What's the difference?" she asked.

"No difference," grunted the butcher. "Some people like to pay fifty cents a pound, some like to pay a dollar!"

Vice-Presidency

1043. Reporters continually probed President George Bush concerning the qualifications and ability of his Vice-President, Dan Quayle. Mr. Quayle's educational background, military service record, and golf game were frequent topics of conversation. However, the President continued to support his Vice-Presidential choice. Following the first "100" days of office, Bush was once again bombarded with the familiar question, "How do you feel now about Dan Quayle assuming Presidential responsibilities in your absence?" Tired of this line of questioning, Bush maintained his sense of humor and responded in stride, "There's no need concerning yourself with the possibility. It will happen over my dead body."

Vocational aptitude

1044. *Vocational advisor to youth:* "Your vocational aptitude test indicates that your best opportunities lie in a field where your father holds an influential position."

Vote—Votes—Voting

1045. A farmer was detained for questioning about an elections scandal. "Did you sell your vote?" the U.S. Attorney asked.

"No sirree, not me," the farmer protested. "I voted for that there fella 'cause I liked him."

"C'mon, now," threatened the attorney. "I have good evidence that he gave you twenty dollars."

"Well, now," the farmer said, "it's plain common-sense that when a feller gives ya twenty dollars ya like him."

W

Wages

1046. A shrewd robber, who suddenly appeared at the paymaster's window of a large plant, demanded: "Never mind the payroll, Bud, just hand over the welfare fund, the group insurance premiums, the pension fund, and the withholding taxes."

1047. One of the neatest ways of asking the boss for a raise in pay was the approach used by John Kieran when he was the sports columnist of the New York *Times.* Feeling the need for more dough but wanting to be tactful about it, Kieran went to his employer, Adolph Ochs, and said respectfully, "Mr. Ochs, working for the *Times* is a luxury I can no longer afford."
He got the raise.

1048. A farmer, in great need of extra hands at haying time, finally asked the town's character if he could help him out.
"What'll ye pay?" asked the good-natured citizen.
"I'll pay what you're worth," replied the farmer.
He scratched his head a minute, then said, "I won't work for that!"

1049. A Nevadan, visiting New York for the first time, stopped a youngster on the street and offered him a dollar if he would show him the way to a certain bank. The boy complied, left the Westerner at the entrance to the bank, and stuck out his hand for the money.
The visitor reached for his wallet and commented that the boy had probably never earned a dollar that easily in all his life.

"Sure, mister," agreed the youngster, "but don't forget that us bank directors in New York is paid high!"

1050. A company was having its annual dinner for the 25-year employees, and the boss had stepped up to the refreshment stand. A worker, fortified by a few trips to the same stand, decided now was the time to hit the chief up for a raise.

So he walked over to the chief executive, stuck out his chin and stated bluntly:

"Mr. Jones, I've worked 25 years for you. I've worked so hard and so conscientiously I've ruined my health."

"I know you have, Smith," the boss answered, and raising his glass he said dramatically: "Here's to your health!"

1051. "Hey boss," Joe nervously began, "I've been working here for more than four years and still don't get paid what I am worth."

"You have a good point," responded the business owner, "and I believe everyone should get paid what they are worth—no matter how large of a cut in pay you will have to take."

Warning

1052. "I'd like to bring Bill home to dinner tonight," the man telephoned his wife.

"To dinner tonight!" she screamed. "You have got to be kidding. You know that the cook just left, I've got a cold, baby's cutting his teeth, the furnace is broken and the butcher won't give us any more credit until we pay up. . ."

"I know," the husband interrupted quietly. "That's why I want to bring him. The poor fool is thinking of getting married."

1053. The young minister was in the pulpit for the first time and she was a little nervous. She read the text: "Behold I Come." The sermon was to follow immediately, but her mind went blank, and she repeated the text: "Behold I Come," hoping to remember the opening words of the sermon—but with no success. Trying to be nonchalant, she leaned forward as she repeated the text for the third time. Under her weight the pulpit gave way and she landed in the lap of one of the elders. "I'm awfully sorry," she said much embarrassed. "I really didn't mean for this to happen."

The man smiled kindly and replied, "Oh, that's all right. I should have been ready after you warned me three times."

Wealth

1054. The world might never have heard of Voltaire as a writer if he hadn't been a math whiz. Taking advantage of a government miscalculation in issuing a national lottery, he formed a syndicate and bought up every ticket. His share made him independent and gave him time to write. His success was assured by the Paris censors, who always banned his books and closed his plays.

1055. A certain nobility had a valet who was violently opposed to the capitalistic system, and who devoted most of his spare time to attending meetings where he could listen while communistic theories were expounded. The master was tolerant because the servant was diligent in the performance of his duties. Suddenly the valet stopped going to meetings, and after several weeks the master became curious enough to ask the reason.

"At the last meeting I attended," said the good man, "it was proved that if all the wealth in the country were divided equally among all the people, the share of each person would be two thousand francs."

"So what?" asked the master.

"Well, I have five thousand francs."

1056. The New York humor magazine *Spy* conducted an investigation to determine the cheapest person in the world. The creative minds behind this project established a phony clearinghouse—the kind of place that sends refund checks when you purchase soap, toothpaste, motor oil, for example—and then issued checks to some of the richest people in America.

The first check, in the amount of $1.56, was returned by more than two dozen people. The checks continued to be sent and returned but they also shrunk in size. The winner of their cheapskate award went to billionaire Donald Trump who endorsed and cashed a $0.13 check.

1057. A small-town pastor was being honored for 40 years of service. Following a banquet, the minister was asked to recall the most memorable moments in his career.

"The most memorable," he began, "was a wedding service I conducted in a roadside chapel. I asked those wishing to be wed in holy matrimony to please come forward. To my surprise, three single women, one widow, and two single men came forward."

Wearing apparel. See Attire

Wedding anniversary

1058. The most impressive evidence of tolerance is a golden wedding anniversary.

Winning/Losing

1059. The desire for victory and agony of defeat is depicted in a "Peanuts" cartoon in which Charlie Brown, after striking out again is consoled by Lucy. "That's all right, Charlie Brown. You win some. You lose some." Charlie Brown replies, "That would be wonderful!"

Witness—Witnesses

1060. The attorney demanded severely, "You testify that you saw the defendant strike the complaining witness, and yet you were three blocks away. Just how far can you see, anyhow?"

"Oh, I don't know exactly," the witness drawled, "about a million miles, I expect—just how far away is the moon?"

1061. "Mr. Witness, you're not telling the same story now that you did right after the shooting happened, are you?"

"No, sir."

"Well, how do you explain the difference?"

"Well," replied the witness, "I was talkin' then; I'm swearin' now."

Woman—Women

1062.   A reporter was interviewing Sir Winston Churchill. "What do you say, Sir," he asked, "to the prediction that in the year 2000, women will be ruling the world?"

Churchill smiled his wise old cherub smile, "They still will, eh?"

1063.   A young sophomore arrived home breathlessly to announce that she had received the first of a new type of comprehensive report card at high school.

"It's got all kinds of statistics and stuff on it," she informed her mother as she handed it over for inspection. "Look at this," she exclaimed, pointing to one particular item. "They gave me an 'F' in sex and I didn't even know I was taking it."

Work

1064.   An executive was having difficulty with her secretary. She decided to confront her shoddy performance. "Nancy," she began, "you don't seem to be into your work. The letters you type are full of errors, rarely do you get to work on time, and why don't you ever answer the phone?"

"The answer to the last part is easy," the secretary responded. "I quit answering the phone because nine times out of ten, it's for you!"

1065.   "How's your new office job?" asked a friend.
"I quit."
"Why?"
"There are several reasons," she answered. "The unfriendliness, sloppy work, terrible language . . . my boss just wouldn't put up with it."

1066.   So you want a day off?!
Let's take a moment to look at what you are asking for.
There are 365 days available for work.
There are 52 weeks per year,
Of which you already have 2 days off each weekend,
Leaving 261 days left for work.

Since you spend 16 hours each day away from work,
That accounts for 170 days.
There are 91 days available for work.
You spend 30 minutes each day on breaks.
That accounts for 23 days each year.
Leaving 68 days available for work.
You spend one hour a day for lunch.
That accounts for another 46 days per year.
Leaving 22 days available for work.
You spend 2 days per year on sick leave.
Leaving 20 days available for work.
You take 9 holidays per year,
Leaving 11 days available for work.
You take 10 days vacation each year.
Leaving 1 day left available for work.
No way are you going to take that day off.

Source Unknown

1067. Sign in a workaholic's office: "THANK GOD IT'S MONDAY!"

1068. A manufacturing conglomerate launched a major campaign to reduce manufacturing errors, increase customer satisfaction, and double their production rate. As employees entered their work area on the first day after the announcement, a large sign had been hung conveying management's commitment. It read:

"To err is human, to forgive divine—neither of which is the policy of this company."

1069. Secretary of Commerce, Malcolm Baldridge enjoyed telling how a high-ranking official responded to an employee's request for a raise by saying: "Because of the influctuational predisposition of your position's productive capacity as juxtaposed to government standards, it would be monetarily injudicious to advocate an increment."

Confused, the employee said, "I don't get it."

The supervisor responded, "That's right."

World, The

1070. If the world is getting smaller, why do they keep raising postal rates?

1071. "I'll make a suit for you," agreed Ben, an overworked tailor, "but it won't be ready for 30 days."

The customer was shocked. "Thirty days," he protested. "Why, the good Lord only took 6 days to create the entire world."

"True," the tailor agreed, "but have you a taken a good look at it lately?"

Worry—Worries

1072. *Contractor:* "Did you hear about Willard, the bank cashier, stealing fifty-thousand and running away with his friend's wife?"

Engineer: "Good heavens! Who'll teach his Sunday school class tomorrow?"

1073. A man was complaining of insomnia. "Even counting sheep is no good. I counted 10,000, sheared 'em, combed the wool, had it spun into cloth, made into suits, took 'em into town—and lost $21 on the deal. So I haven't slept for a week."

1074. The fighter, after taking the full count in a late round of a brawl, finally came to as his trainers worked over him in the dressing room. As his head cleared and he realized what had happened, he said to his manager: "Boy, did I have him worried in the third round! He thought he'd killed me."

Y

Youth

1075.   During a rehearsal of one of his plays, a famous writer became increasingly irritated with the producer's young son, who was convinced that he knew it all.

Repeatedly, the youth interrupted the proceedings to criticize one of the actors. After one such outburst, the playwright turned to him and said:

"My boy, you will have to be more patient with us. After all we are not young enough to know everything."

1076.   An explorer was describing some of his adventures before a high school assembly.

"Suddenly, I came upon a tribe of wild teenagers," he said, "who strangely enough, had no tongues."

"Heavens! No tongues?" exclaimed one student. "How could they talk!"

"They couldn't," said the adventurer. "That's what made them wild."

DEFINITIONS

A

1. Abstract art: the proof that things are not as bad as they are painted to be.

2. Adolescence-Middle age: Adolescence: when you think you will live forever; Middle age: when you wonder how you have lasted so long.

3. Adolescence: a painful period of life—for parents.

4. Adult education: a strenuous effort to learn about things that bored you when you were still young enough to profit from them.

5. Advice: the only commodity where the supply always exceeds the demand.

6. Aging: middle age is when you make each day count. Old age is when you ask for a recount.

7. Allergic reaction: response to an undesirable job.

8. Aloha: the sound you hear when someone with a deep voice laughs.

9. Amateur Carpenter: one who measures once and ends up cutting twice.

10. Apartment building: a place where the landlord and the tenant are both trying to raise the rent.

11. Apprehension, Groundless: See Groundless apprehension.

12. Archaeologist: a person whose career lies in ruins.

13. Archaeology: the science of digging around to find another civilization to blame ours on.

14. Art, Abstract. See Abstract art.

15. Astronaut: one who is glad to be down and out.

16. Attic: a place to store what you will never use until after you sell them at the next garage sale.

17. Autobiography: an accurate representation of the author's inaccurate recollection.

18. Automotive Placement Engineer: parking lot attendant.

19. Average: the poorest of the good and the best of the bad.

B

20. B.A.: a degree which indicates that the holder has mastered the first two letters of the alphabet. . .backwards.

21. Backseat driver: a driver who drives the driver.

22. Balanced meal: one from which the diner has a fifty-fifty chance of recovery.

23. Bank stick-up: unauthorized withdrawal.

24. Balanced budget: when the number of people owed and the number of people paid is equal.

25. Banker: a person who lends you his umbrella when the sun is shining and wants it back the minute it rains.—*Mark Twain*

26. Banquet: an affair at which a person may insist that they aren't much of a speaker, then gets up and spends an hour and a half trying to prove it.

27. Bargain: something you figure out a use for after you've bought it.

28. Baseball: a pane killer.

29. Baseball dugout: a whine cellar.

30. Baseball umpire: See Umpire.

31. Bathing suit: a garment cut to see level.

32. Bathroom scale: a small household appliance commonly used to measure one's feet.

33. Black eye: a stamp of disapproval.

34. Bookie: one who makes his living off bet bugs.

35. Bore: 1. a person, who, if you ask him what time it is, will start to tell you how to make a watch. 2. a person who takes her time taking your time. 3. one who need not repeat himself because he gets it trite the first time. 4. a person who is too generous with her time.

36. Bore: someone who, when you ask them what they think, tell you everything they know.

37. Borrower: a person who always wants to be left a loan.

38. Boss: 1. one who'll raise the roof before they'll raise your salary. 2. the one who watches the clock during the coffee break.

39. Bottoms up: a common experience for an inexperienced sailor.

40. Boxing: guided muscle.

41. Bum: a person-about-town.

42. Bumblebee: a humbug.

43. Bumper crop: pedestrians who land in the hospital because of automobile accidents.

44. Buoyant: ant family's male species.

45. Business: what people go out of when they haven't got any.

46. Buzz words: the official language of insects.

C

47. Candidate, Political: a modest person who shrinks from the publicity of private life to seek the obscurity of public office.

48. Catastrophe: the type of event that gives failure a bad name.

49. Census Taker: one who goes from house to house increasing the population.

50. Champion: one who gets licked two or three times a week and keeps right on calling themself a champion.

51. Change: an event enjoyed most by wet babies.

52. Chaperoning: a spectator spoil-sport.

53. Chess: 1. a game requiring patience, a mathematical mind, and a suit with two pairs of pants. 2. a game played on squares by squares.

54. Chiropractor: a doctor who works their fingers to the bone. . .yours.

55. Christmas: 1. that time of the year when mother has to separate the man from the toys. 2. that time of the year when both trees and parents get trimmed, and sometimes get lit up, too. 3. a season of anticipation, preparation, recreation, relation, prostration and recuperation.

56. Clockwise: an intelligent time-keeper.

57. Cocktail party: where you make new old friends.

58. College: an institution where you learn how to use punctuation marks, but not what to put between them.

59. College professor: one who gets what's left over after the football coach is paid off.

60. Communism: 1. the cause that suppresses. 2. socialism with a gun to make you take it.

61. Commuter: one who shaves and takes a train; and then rides back to shave again.

62. Complex decision: when your two favorite T.V. programs are on at the same time on different channels.

63. Compromise: listening to your spouse's opinion and deciding he/she is right.

64. Computer illiterate: the person using white-out on the screen.

65. Computer illiterate: a person whose display screen is covered with correction fluid.

66. Confidence: that quality which permits an individual to do crossword puzzles with a fountain pen.

67. Confirmed bachelor: a man with no wife expectancy.

68. Con man: one who believes people are all right—if you know how to take them.

69. Conscience: something that no's what's wrong.

70. Cosmetics: applied art.

71. Copy machine: an expert in reproduction.

72. Credit card: the greatest development since the invention of the big wheel.

73. Customer service: what you get when your tip is big enough.

D

74. Daily double: work and slave.

75. Dance school: Disco Tech.

76. Dark corner: a place where people get bright ideas.

77. Dead Sea: unused water bed.

78. Debate: what an avid fisher never forgets.

79. Dentist: one who "tickles the ivories."

80. Diaper: a changeable seat cover.

81. Diary: penned-up emotion.

82. Dieter: 1) a person who goes to great lengths to avoid great widths. 2) one who takes off tomorrow what they put on today.

83. Diploma: a job-hunting license.

84. Diplomacy: 1. the art of saying nothing nicely. 2. the art of saying something when you have nothing to say, or of saying nothing when you have something to say.

85. Diplomat: one who can keep their shirt on while getting something off their chest.

86. Discharged record spinner: a slipped disc jokey.

87. Discretion: when you are sure that you are right but still ask your spouse.

88. Dishonorable: any action practiced by your competitor.

89. Divorce: a splitting headache.

90. Doghouse: falling-out shelter.

91. Dogma: a canine parent.

92. Do-it-yourself enthusiast: a varnishing American.

93. Domestic harmony: music produced only if one person plays second fiddle.

94. Double-crosser: one who acts like a skunk and hopes nobody will get wind of it.

95. Dragon: what dull events do.

96. Dreams: the fool ideas of the day before yesterday that have become the commonplace miracles of today.

97. Drinking: something which makes one lose one's inhibitions and give exhibitions.

98. Driver, Backseat: See Backseat driver.

99. Drug, Miracle: See Miracle drug.

100. Dude ranch: where a person who is rich enough to drive a Cadillac rides a horse.

101. Dugout, Baseball: See Baseball dugout.

E

102. Easy street: the route of all evil.

103. Eavesdropper: a person who loves to listen in, but not as much as they love to talk out.

104. Ecology Engineer: garbage collector.

105. Economist: one who can save money by cutting down some other person's expense.

106. Education: 1. what you have left over when you subtract what you've forgotten from what you learned. 2. a technique employed to open minds so that they may go from cocksure ignorance to thoughtful uncertainty.

107. Egotism: self-intoxication.

108. Electrocardiograph: ticker tape.

109. Epitaph: a monumental lie.

110. Evolution: what makes the chimpanzee in the zoo ask: "Am I my brother's keeper?"

111. Excessively compulsive: compulsively exceeding impulses for excess.

112. Executive: a person who follows a work scedule to a tee.

113. Experience: what you imagine you have until you get more.

114. Expert: one who knows all the answers, if you ask the right questions.

115. Expert: one who will know tomorrow why the things he predicted yesterday didn't happen today.

F

116. Failure: one who never puts things over because they are always putting things off.

117. Failures: the battle scars of those who tried.

118. Farmer, U. S. variety: the only person who can lose money every year, live well, educate children, and then die rich.

119. Fear: the lengthened shadow of ignorance.

120. Fence: the difference between one yard and two yards.

121. Financial wizard: a person who doesn't need some extra money at Christmas time.

122. Flashlight: a mechanical device used by people to carry around dead batteries.

123. Flatterer: one who convinces you that you are not alone in the way you feel about yourself.

124. Forced laughter: what voluntarily occurs when the boss tells a joke.

125. Fore: a golf bawl.

126. Fox: a chicken who gets a mink from a wolf.

127. Fox hunting: the unspeakable after the uneatable.

G

128. Garage sale: selling odds to meet ends.

129. Genius: 1. a crackpot who hit the jackpot. 2. a parent who can help their kids do their homework. 3. someone shrewd enough and lazy enough to do the things right the first time.

130. Go light: optimist's version of a stoplight.

131. Golf: a certain something that depreciates when it's above par.

132. Golfer: one who hits and tells.

133. Good breeding: that quality that enables a person to wait in well-mannered silence while the loud mouth gets the service.

134. Good neighbor: one who makes noise at the same time you make yours.

135. Good toastmaster: one who knows when to pop up and when to pop down.

136. Gossip: 1. one who usually gets caught in their own mouthtrap. 2. cheat-chat. 3. something heard over the sour grapevine.

137. Gossip columnist: one who writes other's wrongs.

138. Graduate school: the place where a young scholar goes off their parent's payroll—and on to their spouse's.

139. Grandparent and grandchild: two people sharing the same enemy.

140. Gravedigger: the last person in the world to let you down.

141. Grouch: one who distrusts people who flatter them and dislikes people who don't.

142. Groundless apprehension: that uneasy feeling right after the plane takes off.

H

143. Harmony, Domestic: See Domestic harmony.

144. H-bomb: an invention to end all inventions.

145. Headache: aspirin deficiency.

146. Highbrow: a person who can listen to the *William Tell* overture without thinking of the *Lone Ranger.*

147. High risk: surgeon operating on a malpractice attorney.

148. Holy rollers: ministerial association-sponsored bowling league.

149. Home: a place a person goes to raise a fuss because something went wrong at the office.

150. Hometown: where people wonder how you became as successful as you are.

151. Homework: skull-drudgery.

152. Hooky: when a small child lets their mind wander—and then follows it.

153. Horn of plenty: located in the car behind you.

154. Horse: an oatsmobile.

155. Hospital: a place where people who are run down wind up.

156. Human being: a person who'll laugh over a family album, then look into a mirror and never crack a smile.

157. Human brain: a wonderful mechanism that starts functioning the minute you get up in the morning and doesn't stop until you get to the office.

158. Humility: the ability to act ashamed when you tell people how wonderful you are.

159. Humor: 1. emotional chaos remembered in tranquility. 2. a smoke screen that keeps us from being blinded by the truth.

160. Hunting, Fox: See Fox hunting.

161. Hypochondria: an illness in which the more you think, the more you think you need a doctor.

162. Hypochondriac: a person who always broods over their health, but never hatches a remedy.

163. Hypocrite: a guy who isn't himself on Sundays.

164. Hypodermic needle: a sick shooter.

I

165. Ideal diet: one that takes off five pounds for good intentions.

166. Ideal weight: the weight listed on people's driver's license.

167. Impossible: what nobody can do until somebody does it.

168. Impossibility: making birth control retroactive.

169. Impossibility: getting your name off a mailing list.

170. Impressario: the only person who never suffers in the long run.

171. Income tax: the first touch of spring.

172. Infinity: a kind of foreverness that begins when a speaker says, "and in conclusion."

173. Inflation: a period when two can live as steeply as one.

174. Information: how army soldiers march.

175. Irritation: attempting to locate a single fly in a dark room.

176. Intellectual: a guy who can keep his mind on a book at a bathing beach.

177. Intersection: a place where two wrongs make a rite.

178. Invest: a word which comes before investigate in the dictionary, but which follows it in practice.

179. Irish: an English-piquing people.

180. Irony: being witty at all costs.

J

181. Jail: the original key club.

182. Juvenile delinquent: a youngster who has been given a free hand but not in the proper place.

K

183. Killing time: suicide on the installment plan.

184. Know-it-all: one who pretends to know something about everything but really knows nothing about anything.

L

185. Las Vegas: 1. a place where people get chip-wrecked. 2. a place where wheels steer people.

186. Laughter: the sound you hear when you spill on yourself or trip over your own two feet.

187. Lawyer: a cat that settles differences between mice.

188. Life: the garment we continually alter but which never seems to fit.

189. Lisp: to call a spade thpade.

190. Listening: silent flattery.

191. Literary tea: a fete worse than death.

192. Long wait: what happens after the nurse tells you to take off your clothes and the doctor will be with you in a minute.

193. Loser: 1) piano player in a marching band. 2) an unopposed political candidate who loses.

194. Loser: a vegetarian who wins a gift certificate from the Beef Producers Association.

195. Low-mileage car: one that wouldn't start for the previous owner.

M

196. Maintenance-free: once broken, the item is irreparable.

197. Marriage: 1. a ceremony where the grocer acquires an account the florist once had. 2. a process whereby love ripens into vengeance. 3. an investment that pays you dividends if you pay interest. 4. oceans of emotions surrounded by expanses of expenses. 5. a very expensive way to get your laundry done free.

198. Masseur: a limberjack.

199. Maternity dress: a kind of magic garment that makes the heir unapparent.

200. Matrimony: the splice of life.

201. Meal, Balanced: See Balanced meal.

202. Mean precipitation: rain falling on Easter bonnets.

203. Middle age: when your past is past.

204. Middle age: that time of your life when your face clears up but your mind goes fuzzy.

205. Middle age: that time in your life when the broad mind and narrow waist exchange places.

206. Minimum: a small mother.

207. Minister: a travel agent for the straight and narrow.

208. Miracle drug: any medicine you can get the kids to take without screaming.

209. Misnomer: the right name for the wrong word.

210. Mixed emotions: the feeling you get when your teenager comes home with an "A" on his or her report card. . .in sex education.

211. Moderns: people who meet a crisis face to face after taking a pill.

212. Modesty: that self-confident feeling that the world already knows or will soon find out.

213. Money: what we spend for luxuries and owe for necessities.

214. Money: the one item that keeps parents in touch with their children.

215. Mounting apprehension: the feeling experienced by pets owned by a taxidermist.

216. Mundane: the day following a heavenly weekend.

217. Music lover, Real: See Real music lover.

N

218. Nature lover: a person who, when treed by a bear, enjoys the view.

219. Nervous people: those who keep the coffee awake at night.

220. Neurotic-Psychotic: Neurotic: a person who builds castles in the air; Psychotic: someone who moves into them.

221. Night gown: a nap sack.

222. Nuclear Physicist: one who has many ions in the fire.

O

223. Obsolescence: what happens to your car once it's paid for.

224. Office picnic: when the boss goes on vacation.

225. Office-seeker: a person who is either appointed or disappointed.

226. Old age: that time of life when you don't care where your spouse goes, just so you don't have to go with them.

227. Old age: when the majority of the names in your address book end with M.D.

228. Old-timer: 1. one who can remember when the village square was a place—not a person. 2. one who can remember when the wonder drugs were mustard plasters and castor oil. 3. one who can remember when you built your garage on top of your house and called it an "attic."

229. One-way conversation: a veterinarian questioning a patient.

230. Onion: a vegetable that builds you up physically but tears you down socially.

231. Optimism: taking out a 30-year home mortgage at age 93.

232. Optimist: one who, when she falls in the soup, considers herself in the swim.

233. Optimist, True: See True optimist.

234. Orator: an unpopular wind instrument.

235. Originality: a pair of fresh eyes.

P

236. Parking lot attendant: professional fender bender.

237. Parking meter: 1. an automatic device that bets a dollar to your nickel that you can't get back before the red flag flips up. 2. a device that makes you do two hours shopping in one.

238. Parking space: a place occupied by someone already there.

239. Patience: a postponed temper.

240. Patience: the practice of concealing your impatience.

241. Patriotism: the frustration you feel when a foreigner wins the championship.

242. Pedestrian: 1. a parent who didn't think the family had any need for two cars.

243. Pessimist: 1. one who complains about the noise when opportunity knocks. 2. one to whom every year is a good whine year. 3. a mis-fortune teller.

244. Phone booth: where one sees the handwriting on the wall.

245. Physicist, Nuclear: See Nuclear physicist.

246. Pick-pocket: one who is into change.

247. Plagiarism: taking something from someone else and making it worse.

248. Playboy, Society: See Society playboy.

249. Police: the only people who are paid to go around pinching people in the wrong places.

250. Political candidate: See Candidate, Political.

251. Politician: 1. a person who will stand for anything that they think will leave them sitting pretty. 2. a person who works their gums before an election and gums up the works afterward.

252. Politician: a person who is willing to do anything for the working class, except become one of them.

253. Polygon: a dead parrot.

254. Precipitation, Mean: See Mean precipitation.

255. Predicament: when a person doesn't want any more birthdays, but still wants the presents.

256. Preservative: that which makes the life expectancy of food greater than your own.

257. Press agent: one who is willing to put your feat in their mouth.

258. Progress: the continuing effort to make the things we eat, drink and wear as good as we think they used to be.

259. Propaganda: what the other side is lying about.

260. Prosperity: something you feel, fold and forward to Washington.

261. Psychiatrist: a head coach.

262. Psychiatrist's couch: bunk bed.

R

263. Radish: a vegetable that speaks for itself.

264. Ranch, Dude: See Dude ranch.

265. Rarity: good, left-over recipes for caviar.

266. Rash of good luck: what happens when you crossbreed poison ivy with a four-leaf clover.

267. Recession: what happens when the boom is lowered.

268. Refrigerator: where you put dabs of food on dishes you don't want to wash.

269. Repair person: the only one who smiles when everything goes wrong.

270. Repartee: glib and take.

271. Resourceful woman: one who teaches the children to swim while waiting for the plumber.

272. Retired cannibal: one who is fed up with people.

273. Rhetoric: language in white tie, hat, and tails.

274. Rural areas: those backward places that use a substance called money rather than credit cards.

S

275. Sales talk: trade wind.

276. School, Graduate: See Graduate school.

277. Secret: something a person tells everybody not to tell anybody.

278. Self-fulfilling prophecy: putting money away for an emergency.

279. Sense of humor: laughing at an event that would make you angry if it happened to you.

280. Sermon: a moralogue.

281. Shoplifting: free enterprise.

282. Shopping mall: amusement park for adults.

283. Short: one whose stature results in their cowboy boots rubbing under their armpits.

284. Silence: the only thing that can't be misquoted.

285. Small talk: that which tends to come out of big mouths.

286. Small town: 1. a place where nothing happens every minute. 2. a place where a person with a private phone is considered anti-social.

287. Small town: 1) where the airport is mowed twice a week. 2) when you write a check on the wrong bank and it covers for you. 3) when fourth street is on the edge of town. 4) when you return home from a weekend visit and it appears in the social column of the local newspaper. 5) when you call the local grocery store and have your groceries delivered to your home. . .and charged.

288. Smuggler: one who neglects his duty to his country.

289. Snob: a person who invents ancestors who would have been ashamed of him if they had been real.

290. Snow: mother nature's white-out.

291. Society playboy: a cashanova.

292. Soft soap: a sort of make-up cream.

293. Spanking: stern punishment.

294. Spare tire: the one you check after you have a flat.

295. Specialist: a generalist with a smaller practice and a larger home.

296. Spring fever: the disinclination of the sap to rise.

297. Stalemate: a husband or wife with one joke.

298. Statistician: a person who believes that if you put your head in a furnace and your feet in a bucket of iced water, on the average you should feel reasonably comfortable.

299. Status quo: Latin for "the mess we're in."—*Ronald Reagan*

300. Stoplight: a place where the cautious and the reckless meet.

301. Strategic misrepresentation: a lie.

302. Stressed: wired and tired.

303. Strip-teaser: one who makes a bare living.

304. Success: 1. the realization of the estimate which you place upon yourself. 2. the good fortune that comes from aspiration, desperation, perspiration, and inspiration.

305. Successful person: one who can lay a firm foundation with the bricks that others throw at them.

306. Summer: that time of the year when you feel so lazy, you can't get out of your own way.

307. Summertime: when parents pack off their troubles to an old Indian camp and smile, smile, smile!

308. Super-seller: one who can convince senior citizens to sign up for maternity benefits.

309. Sympathy: what one usually gives to a friend or relative when they don't want to lend them money.

T

310. Tabloid: a screamlined newspaper.

311. Tax, Income: See Income tax.

312. Tea, Literary: See Literary tea.

313. Telephone: an invention that allows teenagers to go steady without kissing.

314. Television set: a watching machine.

315. Tension: the price you pay for being a race horse instead of a plow horse.

316. Theory: 1. an educated hunch; 2. an impractical plan for doing the impossible.

317. Thunder: drum role in the symphony of life.

318. Time, Killing: See Killing time.

319. Tire, Spare: See Spare tire.

320. Toastmaster: the person between the meal and the speaker who tries to pretend that the latter won't be as much torture as the former.

321. Toastmaster, Good: See Good toastmaster.

322. Tolerance: letting other people find happiness in their way instead of your way.

323. Tombstone: a grave situation.

324. Trade deficit: when people borrow one more item than they return.

325. True optimist: one who always has her bad breaks relined.

U

326. Umpire: the original strike arbitrator.

327. Undertaker: one who signs all their correspondence, "eventually yours."

328. Unemployed jester: nobody's fool.

329. Upward adjustment: product price increase.

V

330. Vacation: 1. a change of routine that makes you feel good enough to go back to work and poor enough to have to. 2. a brief relief without the chief.

331. Vacuum: electric broom with a stomach.

332. Video games: garbage disposal for quarters.

333. Vision: looking farther than you can see.

334. Vitamin: what you do when a visitor rings the doorbell.

W

335. Wastebasket: something to throw things near.

336. Wedding rehearsal: aisle trial.

337. Wedding ring: a warhoop.

338. Weight gain: moving into a larger slacks bracket.

339. Widowhood: the proof that women live longer than men.

340. Wig: a convertible top.

341. Will contest: heir splitting.

342. Wisdom: knowing the difference between pulling your weight and throwing it around.

343. Woman: 1. a delusion men like to hug. 2. a creature who is either making a fool out of a man, or making a man out of a fool.

344. Woman, Resourceful: See Resourceful woman.

345. Woodpecker: a knocking bird.

346. World history: scrap book.

Y

347. Yacht: a floating debt.

348. Yawn: opening one's mouth and wishing that others would close theirs.

349. Youth: a good substitute for experience.

350. Yuppie accident: a Saab story.

GENERAL INDEX

(Numbers in the index refer to selections
in the text, not to page numbers)

A

Abbreviation, Abbreviations, 657
Abdomen, 276
Absence, 197, 201, 280, 293
Absent-mindedness, 1
Abuse-Abusiveness, 693
Acceleration, 22
Accelerator, 165
Accent-Accents, 708
Accident-Accidents, 403
Accident, Automobile, 588
Accomplishment, Accomplishments, 981
Accord, 469
Accountant, Accountants, 501
Accuracy, 2, 3
Accusation-Accusations, 169
Achievement-Achievements, 4–7, 981
Acquaintance, New,-Acquaintances, New, 402
Action, 117
Actor-Actors, 180, 953
Actor's Club, 156
Actress-Actresses, 590
Adams, John Quincy, 735
Addition (Mathematics), 41
Address, Addresses, 973
Adenauer, Konrad, 25
Admiral-Admirals, 619

Admiration, 8
Admission, Guilt, 991
Advancement, 9, 323
Advance Payment, 452
Advantage, Advantages, 817
Advertisement-Advertisements, 391, 464, 710
Advertising, 10–14, 336, 956
Advice, 73, 80, 524, 688, 852
Advisor, Vocational, 1044
Africa, 456, 516, 650
After-dinner speaker-After-dinner speakers, 794
Age, 15–20, 363, 609, 842, 1143
Agent, Insurance-Agents, insurance, 511
Aging, 21–26, 781
Agriculture, 174
Aim, 291
Air-conditioning, 33
Airplane, Airplanes, 639
Airport-Airports, 451, 639, 1016
Air travel, 1016
Alarm clock, Alarm clocks, 353
Alcoholic liquor, 26, 38, 93, 99, 101, 194, 288, 326, 624, 661, 815, 886
Alimony, 591
Allegation, Allegations, 531
Allen, George E., 734
Allen, John, 724

251

Movie director-Movie directors, 622
Movies, Talking, 520
Moving man-Moving men, 521
Mule-Mules, 1005, 1008
Mule, Army,-Mules, Army, 733
Munich, Germany, 625
Murder-Murders, 489, 715
Music, 593, 652, 653, 712
Musical instrument-Musical instruments, 8, 612
Musician-Musicians, 8, 522, 652, 653
Mustache-Mustaches, 1037
Mutilation, 423
Mystery-Mysteries, 665, 917

N

Nag-Nagging, 329, 393
Nail-Nails, 1004
Name-Names, 79, 347, 438, 480, 654–661, 976, 1018
Name-calling, 438
Napoleon I, 51, 785
Nature, 662, 794
Naval surgeon, 934
Navy, 619
Nazi-Nazis, 251
Necessity-Necessities, 106, 519, 913
Necklace-Necklaces, 779
Necktie-Neckties, 74, 342
Negative proof, 779
Neighbor-Neighbors, 33, 113, 291, 390, 392, 828, 920, 1001
Neighborliness, 388
Nephew-Nephews, 566
Nepotism, 312
Nervousness, 1053
Neurological Institute, 389
Neurosis-Neuroses, 781
Nevada, State of, 1049
Newark, New Jersey, 639
Newcomer-Newcomers, 392
New Deal, 734
New England, 257, 423, 799, 908, 957, 1025, 1042
New Haven, Connecticut, 1025
New Jersey, State of, 483
Newlywed-Newlyweds, 191, 387, 533, 649, 744
New Mexico, State of, 3, 803
Newscaster, Television, 989

Newspaper-Newspapers, 13, 101, 116, 600, 734, 903
Newspaper headline-Newspaper headlines, 657
Newspaperman-Newspapermen, 205
Newspaper office-Newspaper offices, 464
Newspaper reporter-Newspaper reporters, 115, 186
New York, New York, 147, 186, 348, 485, 677, 781, 966, 986, 1000, 1049
New York Times, 734, 1047
Night club-Night clubs, 186, 701
Night school-Night schools, 964
Nobleman-Noblemen, 1055
Noise, 297, 912
Nonchalance, 1053
Non-return, 412
Northerner-Northerners, 100
Nose, 274, 787
Nostalgia, 279
Notice-Notices, 223
Novak, Kim, 280
Nuclear Age, 663, 664
Nudism-Nudity, 274, 665–670
Nudist colony-Nudist colonies, 668
Nuisance-Nuisances, 716
Nurse-Nurses, 129, 299, 615, 703, 767
Nursery-Nurseries, 1032
Nursing home-Nursing homes, 840

O

Oak tree-Oak trees, 343, 1061
Oath-Oaths, 1030
Oatmeal, 814
Obedience, 101, 138, 600
Obesity, 237
Obituary-Obituaries, 115, 734
Objection-Objections, 626, 705
Objective-Objectives, 979
Obliteration, 654
Obstetrics, 615
Occupation-Occupations, 158, 671, 672, 704
Ochs, Adolph, 1047
Odds, 697
Odoriferous, 483
Offense-Offensiveness, 870
Offer, Sales,-Offers, Sales, 709
Office-Offices, 284
Office boy-Office boys, 117, 962

Office experience, 328
Office girl-Office girls, 904
Office Humor, 673
Office manager-Office managers, 317
Office procedure, 328
Officers' Mess, 57
Office staff, 314
Ohio, State of, 284, 1005
Oil field-Oil fields, 357
Oilman-Oilmen, 732, 869
Oil well-Oil wells, 357
Oklahoma, State of, 198
Old age, 395, 609, 992
Old maid-Old maids, 178
Olive-Olives, 282, 470
Olives, Jar of, 470
Omaha, Nebraska, 746
Omen-Omens, 251
Onion-Onions, 537
"On the wagon", 293
Open house, 272
Opening celebration, 272
Opening night-Opening nights, 205
Operation, Surgical, 269, 271, 697, 789
Operator, Switchboard,-Operators,
    Switchboard, 985
Opinion-Opinions, 674, 913, 958
Opponent-Opponents, 198, 556
Opportunity, Business,-Opportunities,
    Business, 1044
Opposition, Political, 626
Orator-Orators, 796
Oregon, State of, 735
Organ-Organs, 522
Orphanage-Orphanages, 672
Ostracism, 201
Ostrich-Ostriches, 733
Outdoors, 854
Outer space, 13, 675–677
Outhouse-Outhouses, 655
Overcoat-Overcoats, 780
Overconfidence, 617
Overvaluation, 34
Overweight, 661, 670, 678–682, 910
Ownership, 113
Oxygen tent-Oxygen tents, 494

P

Paderewski, Ignace, 8
Page one, Newspaper, 734

Pain-Pains, 292, 350, 641, 956
Pain sensitivity, 398
Painter-Painters, 324, 999
Painting, Oil,-Paintings, Oil, 64
Pajamas, 451
Pants, 601
Paper doll-Paper dolls, 99
Parade-Parades, 58
Parent-Parents, 672, 833, 976
Parent-Child, 95, 165, 671, 683–693, 705,
    862, 983, 1021
Parenthood, 783
Paris, France, 67, 170, 1054
Park-Parks, 296
Park bench-Park benches, 343
Parking, 322
Parking lot-Parking lots, 827
Parking space-Parking spaces, 636
Parole, 201
Parson-Parsons, 412
Partnership, 694–696
Party-Parties, 280
Party, Birthday,-Parties, Birthday, 395
Party, Children's, 951
Party, Cocktail,-Parties, Cocktail, 456
Party line, Political, 173
Pass, Military, 46
Past, The, 875
Pasteurized milk, 495
Pastor-Pastors, 812, 916
Paternal influence, 1044
Paternalism, 27
Patience, 152, 1075
Patient, Hospital,-Patients, Hospital, 129,
    484
Pay deduction-Pay deductions, 333
Paymaster's window, 1046
Payment-Payments, 200, 221, 236, 290,
    741, 761
Payment, Advance, 452
Payment, Installment, 506
Payola, 972
Payroll-Payrolls, 1046
Peanut-Peanuts, 127, 713, 917
Pedestrian-Pedestrians, 511
Pedigree, 28
Penalty-Penalties, 94
Penitentiary-Penitentiaries, 79, 672
Penmanship, 4
"Penny," 661
Penny-Pennies, 638, 682